Internet Turnaround

The use of internet marketing
to turnaround company

Published in 2007 by
Corporate Turnaround Centre Pte Ltd.

Printed in Singapore
by Markono Print Media Pte Ltd.

9 8 7 6 5 4
09 08

TABLE OF CONTENTS

Dr Mike Teng is the author of the book *"Corporate Turnaround: Nursing a sick company back to health"*, in 2002 which is also translated into the Bahasa Indonesia. It was one of the top selling management books then. In 2006, he authored another book entitled, *"Corporate Wellness: 101 Principles in Turnaround and Transformation."* Both of these books are translated into Mandarin. He also published in 2007 three books, namely entitled: *Internet Turnaround: The Use of Intersnet Marketing to Turnaround Companies, Training Manual: Corporate Turnaround and Transformation Methodology and Link Baiting to Improve Your Page Ranking on Search Engines.*

He has been interviewed on the national media on many occasions on the subject of corporate turnaround and transformation. Dr Teng is widely recognized as a turnaround CEO in Asia by the news media such as the Channel NewsAsia, News Radio FM 93.8, the Boss Magazine, Economic Bulletin, the Today, World Executive Digest, Lianhe ZaoPao, StarBiz and the Straits Times.

Dr Teng is currently the Managing Director of a UK multinational company based in Singapore, responsible for the Asia Pacific region. He has 500 staff reporting into him.

He has 27 years of experience in corporate turnaround, strategic planning and operational management responsibilities in the Asia Pacific region. Of these, he held Chief Executive Officer's positions for 17 years in multi-national, local and publicly listed companies. He led in the successful turnaround of several troubled companies.

Dr Teng served as the Executive Council member for fourteen years and the last four years as the President of the Marketing Institute of Singapore (2000 - 2004), the national body representing individual and corporate members in Singapore. Dr Teng holds a Doctor in Business Administration (DBA) from the University of South Australia, Master in Business Administration (MBA) and Bachelor in Mechanical Engineering (BEng) from the National University of Singapore. He is also a Professional Engineer (P Eng, Singapore), Chartered Engineer (C Eng, UK) and Fellow Member of Chartered Institute of Marketing (FCIM), Chartered Management Institute (FCMI), Institute of Mechanical Engineers (FIMechE), Institute of Electrical Engineers (FIEE), Marketing Institute of Singapore (FMIS) and Senior Member of Singapore Computer Society (SMSCS).

Ewen Chia Asia's #1 Online Business Consultant

Graduated from Singapore Institute of Management, Ewen Chia holds a B(Sc) Management Honors degree. After graduation, he held a full time sales and marketing job struggling to make ends needs just like every working person.

Striving to earn an extra income, Ewen started learning and experimenting with an internet business in 1997. **For a full 5 years, he worked on his business every single day from 11pm - 3am while still holding a full time day job.**

He was motivated to succeed to build a better life for his family and to clear mounting credit card debts. After years of perseverance, learning and very little sleep, Ewen was finally able to make a fortune online from 2002. From his experience and expertise as an internet entrepreneur, Ewen set up **Autopilot Internet Income Pte Ltd** to provide **proven training** and advice on Internet Marketing to both aspiring individual internet entrepreneurs and companies. The core mission of **Autopilot Internet Income Pte Ltd** is to promote and encourage Internet entrepreneurship around the world as a medium for individuals and companies to make extra income and profits.

Ewen honestly believes that anyone who's willing to put in the effort will be able to achieve **complete financial freedom** using the Internet. The success stories and testimonials of his many students speak for themselves.

Ewen Chia's Personal Success Story:

Ewen is an early Internet business pioneer who has been marketing on the internet since 1997.

As a world famous and highly-respected marketer, Ewen is often called upon for his ingenious marketing advice - especially in the areas of business integration, profit leverage, product creation and online branding.

Ewen Chia is known as the **"World's #1 Super Affiliate"** and his name is synonymous with Affiliate Marketing.

Widely acknowledged as the secret weapon of many other Internet Marketing experts, Ewen has an uncanny ability to trounce the competition and take on the coveted #1 reseller spot in almost every marketing rollout.

Ewen is a rare breed because he actually makes thousands of dollars online every single day. A brand new internet business he set up recently netted over _**US$100,000.00 in less than 30 days in March 2007**_.

Another internet business generated a whopping **US$1.497 MILLION in just 36 hours** and he did it without spending a cent on advertising or promotion.

Ewen has taught thousands of students worldwide using his proprietary Autopilot Internet Income™ System which allows anyone to make a fulltime income purely from the Internet. Ewen has more than *300,000+ subscribers* purchasing his products.

Many have been able to quit their day jobs, live the internet lifestyle and achieve real financial freedom thanks to his proven teachings and strategies.

Ewen is also a much sought after **international speaker** and has toured the world sharing his Internet business knowledge and experience.

He has worked extensively with Adam Khoo Learning Technologies Group Pte Ltd, Success Resources Pte Ltd, the World Internet Summit and many others.

In November 2006 (Singapore), Ewen received the **World Internet Summit "World Internet Challenge"** award for starting a new Internet business and making over **US$80,000.00 in 3 days LIVE** right in front of an amazed audience of 1,000 participants.

In March 2007 (Australia), Ewen was unanimously voted the **Best Speaker** by the 350 strong audience at the **World Internet Summit.**

VOTED BEST SPEAKER
WORLD INTERNET SUMMIT - AUSTRALIA 2007

Ewen has also been officially invited as the <u>only local featured speaker</u> at the world's biggest internet marketing event - World Internet Mega Summit Singapore in May 2007.

You can see some of Ewen's Internet Marketing products here:

http://www.SecretAffiliateWeapon.com

http://www.AutopilotProfits.com

http://www.AffiliateOfTheMonth.com

Introduction

"The Future belongs to those who prepare for it"

The future of a business rest in the hands of its management; the future belongs to managers who have presence of mind and a broad capacity to think about the next big thing. Think ahead and plan ahead. Be prepared for change. You can never know what to expect but you can prepare for everything. With this as our starting point, we introduce you to the concept of business success in the 21st century. And here you are with a small or medium sized enterprise. You've heard that the Internet is a great marketing tool. You've heard it can change the way you conduct your business. You're not only on the right path, you're also reading perhaps the only book that covers what you need to know to succeed in business online. The business principles and outlined marketing practices will turn your business into a stellar success, no matter what your industry, no matter what your business stage.

If you are looking to maximize the Internet impact for your enterprise then you have the right book in your hands..

The Internet offers immense possibilities for building, promoting, and marketing a business in a very cost-effective and speedy manner. The online environment essentially cuts your overheads. The possibilities are far greater than telephone, television, regular mail, and other communication media simply because the Internet is real-time. It is a live entity, Imagine having access to hundreds and thousands of potential customers all over the world at the click of a mouse! This is the Internet.

The modern Internet is the most powerful tool in your marketing arsenal. This one tool has the ability to turnaround your entire corporate practice. The Internet not only inspires more effective and efficient marketing strategy, it actually changes the way marketing is conducted. It has effectively increased market scope on a global level. There are literally hundreds of businesses trying to find customers all over the world but the markets are so huge, you only need a tiny portion of it to make your business a financial success.

That said, buyer attention is a difficult thing to find and an existing customer is truly a prized possession. The possibilities are unparalleled and indeed exciting but they leave many organizations wondering how to capitalize. Most companies miss the big picture.

First of all: a live website does not guarantee success. You can't assume people will visit your site just because it's on the Internet. Many companies do and they quickly fall into insolvency. You need to define your purpose. The failures of online businesses are mainly due to the avoidance of basic marketing skills and an inability to recognize that the internet is not a marketing concept. Remember, before you make any move in marketing, that the Internet is a medium, a great marketing tool. It's not a marketing concept in itself.

This ebook provides an "Execution Plan" to build an online business and to incorporate Internet Marketing techniques to promote your enterprise. This ebook tells you how to get started with Internet Marketing and takes you through planning and execution phases. It's an "Action Oriented" plan to tell you step by step how to harness the power of Internet and, if need be, turnaround your business. That said, readers with small to medium sized enterpirses, clear fundamental marketing concepts and some prior experience are best poised to appreciate the advice here and benefit from it.

The future of the Internet can be assessed: the total world population using Internet at the moment is less than 15 per cent[1]. Its reach will contine to expand and grow in the future. Having Internet Marketing knowledge will help business owners capitalize on the immense possibilities of the Internet. This ebook aims to do just that – to provide you with the tools you need to win the marketing battle.

Happy Clicking!

---

[1] Source: www.internetworldstats.com

Foreword

Warm up

Why is marketing success crucial to your business? Marketing is what drives any business, including yours. It attracts new leads and contributes to maintaining existing customers. In the ever-evolving world of small enterprises, competition is paramount. It is crucial for businesses to learn creative and innovative marketing techniques to maximize their potential. Customers these days are educated and base their business decisions on a weath of information available on the Internet. They also have an immense number of businesses vying for their attention.

For your Internet-based marketing efforts to succeed, you need innovative techniques to reach out to prospective customers and convince them to buy your product. This might mean completely reworking your marketing strategy. It is imperative to the success of your companiy that you secure new customers and continue to provide your existing ones with a reason to come back.

Marketing is an important part of any business strategy and should be understood at every level of the company. For entry level to management level presonnel, the importance of marketing needs to be emphasized. It is too important a subject to be left under the watch of a single designated department in the company. Every employee must understand that marketing will chart their future, more so than any other factor.

Why the Internet?
On the battlefield, in the heat of the actions, wouldn't you want the best and most advanced weapons available? You may have all the passion to win and the skills to compete but it's the right tools that give you an edge; that dramatically improve your chances of winning.

No matter how qualified the surgeon, he still needs a well-equipped operation theater to operate on a patient. The patient's chances of dying are too high if there is no medicine or equipment available, even if with the best of doctors besides him.

The scenario is very much the same in today's marketing world. Technology has decided to a great extent how we communicate. The modern Personal Computer (PC) is *the* multimedia device that drives communication; from transmitting television signals to webcasting, digital downloads and much more. The PC is also becoming increasingly mobile merging with handheld devices like phones, pocket PCs, and laptops.

The best way to reach customers in the past was a newspaper advert, a flyer, or a television ad, or a cold-call. But all of them have their own disadvantages and fall short of being an all-round marketing tool. The Internet is one such wonderful technology. It is the only technology that is a grand platform for many other technologies of present; holding the promise of a complete turnaround in businesses.

Few Internet Statistics

The following stats from www.internetworldstats.com help us understand the growth of
Internet in Asia

INTERNET USERS AND POPULATION STATISTICS FOR ASIA

ASIA REGION	Population (2006 Est.)	% Pop. of World	Internet Users, Latest Data	Penetration (% Population)	% Usage of World	Use Growth (2000-2006)
Asia Only	3,667,774,066	56.4 %	394,872,213	10.8 %	36.4 %	245.5 %
Rest of the World	2,831,922,994	43.6 %	691,378,690	24.4 %	63.6 %	180.3 %
WORLD TOTAL	6,499,697,060	100.0 %	1,086,250,903	16.7 %	100.0 %	200.9 %

NOTES: (1) Internet Usage and Population Statistics for Asia were updated for Sept. 18, 2006. (2) Population numbers are based on data contained in world gazetteer. (3) The most recent usage comes mainly from data published by Nielsen//NetRatings , ITU , and other local sources. (4) Data on this site may be cited, giving due credit and establishing an active link back to Internet World Stats . (5) For definitions and help, see the site surfing guide. © Copyright 2006, Miniwatts Marketing Group. All rights reserved.

The table below gives country specific data for Asia

ASIA INTERNET USAGE AND POPULATION

ASIA	Population (2006 Est.)	Internet Users, (Year 2000)	Internet Users, Latest Data	Penetration (% Population)	(%) Users in Asia	Use Growth (2000-2006)
Afganistan	26,508,694	-	30,000	0.1 %	0.0 %	n/a %
Armenia	2,967,116	30,000	150,000	5.1 %	0.0 %	400.0 %
Azerbaijan	8,388,479	12,000	678,800	8.1 %	0.2 %	5,556.7 %
Bangladesh	136,138,461	100,000	300,000	0.2 %	0.1 %	200.0 %
Bhutan	796,314	500	25,000	3.1 %	0.0 %	4,900.0 %
Brunei Darussalem	393,568	30,000	56,000	14.2 %	0.0 %	86.7 %
Cambodia	15,017,110	6,000	41,000	0.3 %	0.0 %	583.3 %
China	1,306,724,067	22,500,000	123,000,000	9.4 %	31.1 %	446.7 %
East Timor	947,401	-	1,000	0.1 %	0.0 %	0.0 %
Georgia	4,435,046	20,000	175,600	4.0 %	0.0 %	778.0 %
Hong Kong *	7,054,867	2,283,000	4,878,713	69.2 %	1.2 %	113.7 %
India	1,112,225,812	5,000,000	60,000,000	5.4 %	15.2 %	1,100.0 %
Indonesia	221,900,701	2,000,000	18,000,000	8.1 %	4.6 %	800.0 %
Japan	128,389,000	47,080,000	86,300,000	67.2 %	21.9 %	83.3 %
Kazakhstan	14,711,068	70,000	400,000	2.7 %	0.1 %	471.4 %
Korea, North	23,312,595	-	-	-	-	n/a %

Korea, South	50,633,265	19,040,000	**33,900,000**	67.0 %	8.6 %	78.0 %
Kyrgystan	5,377,484	51,600	**280,000**	5.2 %	0.1 %	442.6 %
Laos	5,719,497	6,000	**25,000**	0.4 %	0.0 %	316.7 %
Macao*	490,696	60,000	**201,000**	41.0 %	0.1 %	235.0 %
Malaysia	27,392,442	3,700,000	**11,016,000**	40.2 %	2.8 %	197.7 %
Maldives	298,841	6,000	**19,000**	6.4 %	0.0 %	216.7 %
Mongolia	2,568,204	30,000	**268,300**	10.4 %	0.1 %	794.3 %
Myanmar	54,021,571	1,000	**78,000**	0.1 %	0.0 %	7,700.0 %
Nepal	25,408,817	50,000	**175,000**	0.7 %	0.0 %	250.0 %
Pakistan	163,985,373	133,900	**10,500,000**	6.4 %	2.7 %	7,741.7 %
Philippines	85,712,221	2,000,000	**7,820,000**	9.1 %	2.1 %	291.0 %
Singapore	3,601,745	1,200,000	**2,421,000**	67.2 %	0.6 %	101.8 %
Sri Lanka	19,630,230	121,500	**280,000**	1.4 %	0.1 %	130.5 %
Taiwan	22,896,488	6,260,000	**13,800,000**	60.3 %	3.5 %	120.4 %
Tajikistan	6,620,008	2,000	**5,000**	0.1 %	0.0 %	150.0 %
Thailand	66,527,571	2,300,000	**8,420,000**	12.7 %	2.1 %	266.1 %
Turkmenistan	6,723,715	2,000	**36,000**	0.5 %	0.0 %	1,700.0 %
Uzbekistan	26,311,197	7,500	**880,000**	3.3 %	0.2 %	11,633.3 %
Vietnam	83,944,402	200,000	**10,711,000**	12.8 %	2.7 %	5,255.5 %
TOTAL ASIA	**3,667,774,066**	**114,303,000**	**394,872,213**	**10.8 %**	**100.0 %**	**245.5 %**

NOTES: (1) The Asian Internet Statistics were updated for Sept. 18, 2006. (2) CLICK on each country name to see detailed data for individual countries and regions. (3) The demographic (population) numbers are based on data contained in world gazetteer. (4) The usage numbers come from various sources, mainly from data published by Nielsen//NetRatings , ITU , and other trustworthy sources. (5) Data may be cited, giving due credit and establishing an active link to Internet World Stats. (6) For definitions and help, see the site surfing guide.

Some people use the Internet to communicate with family and friends; others use it for commerce. For some it's a great entertainment resource. Whatever their particular reason, people ARE hooked to the internet!

The Internet has become a common denominator cutting across societies, age groups and nations. So why not sail your boat in this river – you will surely reach places.

Companies can establish a Marketing System based on the Internet. They can sell products, provide customer service, generate leads, build and promote an online presence and thus help drive business to new heights and dramatically increase customer base. It's surely an opportunity and the challenge is to be able to successfully capitalize on it.

Marketing helps business grow by attracting new customers and keeping old ones. This book will show you how the Internet can help you to do both.

Let's zoom in to start learning the tools to make online success possible.

How To Use This Book

The purpose of this book is to make the internet accessible to every day business professionals. It aims to introduce not only basic theories but also practical schemes for implementation of common internet-based business strategies. Although part of the focus is on the idea of business turnaround – you can use this book to help pull your business out of a financial tail spin and back into solvency – the theories and strategies discussed here can be applied to benefit any online business at any stage of its life.

When you've worked your way through this book, you should be in a position to enjoy considerable online success whatever your online venture happens to involve. You should simply be able to enjoy increased online success by implementing some of the ideas we discuss here. There's nothing to stop you using all of them, but, at the same time, you don't need to use every single idea, letter for letter as it's presented here.

Ideally, you should use this book as both a guide and a reference book for your online business venture. When you first read through these pages, try to simply follow the text. Don't worry about taking notes. Keep in mind only the ideas that strike you. Begin to absorb basic concepts about internet practices like social networking but don't worry too much about figuring out how you can use these types of mediums for your business promotion.

When you've read through the book at least once, now it's time to use it as a reference book. Start to see the potential for advertising success using online practices. Start to think about the specific practices that might work for your business. Now, on your second read through, it's time to start taking notes and building up a working strategy specific for your business.

Remember above all, be creative with your ideas and strategies. Be open-minded and prepared to experiment. This mindset, above all else, will bring you success in business.

Chapter 1: A Winning Marketing Strategy

This book is designed to help entrepreneurs achieve the best possible results for their business using the internet and combining knowledge of this important medium with an understanding of solid business principles.

The businesss advice in this book is particularly selected to help the struggling business owner turn their business from a sure loser into a sure winner. The techniques in this book will help you cut costs and maximize your sales quickly using the internet as your primary medium. If your business is currently failing or on the brink of failure, this book is your lifeline.

There is a need to shift from traditional modes of marketing that were limited to the so called brick and mortar infrastructures to new ones which are more relevant and cost effective to SMEs (Small Medium Enterprises). There is a great need for SMEs to meet existing market competition as well as to carve out new market niches but this is impossible without there first being an affordable method for marketing.

Another major problem for businesses is the use of an incorrect or inexact marketing strategy. When you decide to implement the internet-based marketing techniques explained in this book, you really need to have a precise and effective marketing strategy in place.

The Marketing Strategy
To help you to use this book properly, we have also included in this chapter the groundbreaking marketing strategies used by virtually all successful businesses around the world.

Whether your business is big or small, the following steps will ensure your marketing and business success.

Step One: You Must Identify Your Potential Market Niche
What is niche marketing? What is a niche market? Niche marketing is the process of finding and serving a small but profitable market segment. Generally, niche marketing involves designing products or services specifically for a target market. A niche market is thus the small but profitable market that is, generally an untapped resource. They tend to fall through the cracks of major corporation advertising efforts.

On the Internet, niche marketing is interesting and it is also particularly popular. The Internet has created a fairly level playing field for businesses so niche marketing on the web offers great opportunities for virtually very business. To succeed, all you really need is extensive keyword research and analysis. The good news is, all you need is one talented individual to do this. It doesn't take much and there are lots of free resources at your disposal.

That said, most major companies can pay huge amounts of money to hire professional marketing strategists. For effective branding and market positioning, it is imperative for you and your management team to properly identify your potential market niche.

Some people are under the misconception that it is easy to do this. It's not. And you certainly should not take this process likely. Perhaps the most difficult but critical task, if you misidentify your market niche, your customers and their needs, you are going to have immense problems down the road.

What is a marketing niche?

For both offline and online market, it is important to capture the customers' attention within a short time span. Customers need to be convinced of your expertise and skills. They need to be able to quickly understand your area of business as well as the strengths of your business. Customers think in terms of keywords. Whether they're searching for a product or service online or offline, they will use keywords to identify what they want or need.

Your objective is to capture your customer's keywords in your marketing campaign. When your business is primarily service-oriented, this is even more crucial because your customers are unlikely to come across your business in the first place if you can't identify their keywords and use them in the proper way.

In the online world, it's also more crucial to capture the attention of your prospects quickly. They can click away from the website content within seconds if it does not captivate their attention within that short time span.

The good news is that the Internet does provide free to low-cost resources to enhance marketing efforts, particularly online marketing efforts. For example, www.wordtracker.com enables us to evaluate the effectiveness of selected keywords. This is one of a number of free resources that target ways to identify the potential online market coverage of keywords.

The KEI (Keyword Effectiveness Index) is another resource used to ascertain the effectiveness of selected keywords. The KEI reflects demand and supply of keywords to give you a good insight into how your target customers are searching. As a general rule, a KEI (according to www.wordtracker.com) of less than 10 is not good and you should thus avoid these words. It probably reflects a high number of market players targeting a relatively small pool of demand for a product or service.

Another problem faced by many companies: there is definitely a propensity to use industry jargon words and phrases as keywords. Industry jargon is known as such because it is used in the industry and not used by or perceived by industry outsiders or your targeted customers.

Useful sites to identify market potentials are:
www.inventory.overture.com
www.goodkeywords.com

www.pixelfast.com/overture/
www.google.com
www.ebay.com
www.Big-Boards.com
www.Del.icio.us/
www.icerocket.com

Internet marketing also provides a relatively cheap and effective marketing channel. It offers both a local and global marketing platform. At the same time, the structure of the Internet and daily internet usage dictate the importance of getting onto the first page of search results, not only for the smaller search engines or industry specific search engines. It's most important to get a top ranking for the keyword search results on the most popular search engines, including Google, Yahoo and MSN.. Many companies in the US are competing for top positions on Internet search engines. Their objective is generally to boost their ranking to boost their brand equity. People somehow perceive search engines such as Google to be the government of Internet. If the website appears on the front page of Google, people perceive the companies owing the websites as having higher brand equity.

The primary thrust is to identify a market niche with high demand and low supply. Thereafter, the company can focus on this category or niche by "creating" a leadership position in that niche. Such claims can be highlighted in the corporate tagline (ensure that the claim is defensible/ valid) and formulate offline and online sales/marketing strategies to further reinforce that market leadership position for that identified niche and keyword.

Step Two: You Must Test The Market Niche
Once your market niche is identified, it is important to test its profitability using a survey site. Tools using websites such as www.adwords.google.com, www.payperclickanalyst.com will help you to assess whether the identified potential market niche is viable; whether you can make money from it or not.

You can also get important information about the cost of advertising campaigns, locally and worldwide using sites like AdWords. You can also play out a few different strategies to find out which one works the best. To tap the market properly, you need to have the right campaign to attract your potential customers. Online, the right campaign is all about keywords so test as many of these out as you can to find the ones that work best.

Step Three: You Must Identify the Right Product and Service for Your Market
You need to assess what your customer wants to provide them with a product or service that is going to establish you as their primary source. If they are going to spend money on you, then you're going to have to give them something that satisfies their primary needs. Of course, you should think about the price your customers are willing to pay, the quality they are going to want,

Step Four: You Must Write A Winning Sales Letter

After you've successfully managed to identify the keywords used by your potential market niche, another important step for your marketing efforts is the creation of a good sales letter to put across the most important and interesting details about your product or service. The idea is to attract your customers to your business with good sales copy and a demonstrated keen awareness of what they want and need from your company. Getting the right sales letter can be costly but if it's good enough, your copy will serve as your 24/7 salesperson. Get an expert's help if you think you need it.

Step Five: You Must Build An Attractive Website
For your online business to be a success, you definitely need a website dedicated to it. Your website should be all of these things: easy to build, maintenance-free, low cost, credible, a traffic-builder, and a customer-converter. It's not enough to simply have the right product or service. It's not enough to have your market niche down. Online, you really need to have a website that is going to be focused on your business; that's going to get your potential customers to buy from you and come back to you in the future. While one of the main focuses of this book is the development of winning website content, here are a few additional tips you should keep in mind when you are building your website or having it built.

First of all, your website must be built for speed. Everyone is in a hurry. This is true of internet users just as it's true of people in real life. No one has time to spend having around and there are few things as frustrating when you're on the Internet as a webpage that takes forever to load. You have between 10 and 30 seconds to capture the attention of your potential customer. To minimize your load time, keep graphics small. Compress them where possible. Use flashy technology JavaScript, Flash, Streaming Audio/Video, animation only as it is appropriate and necessary for your presentation. At the very least, minimize its use on your homepage.

Second, you should make sure that your website really targets your audience. This is easier said than done and it's sometimes overlooked. You need to present an image with your website. Reflect your target audience in your site. If you're marketing to clean cut professionals, make sure your site is also clean and professional looking. If you're catering to a young and hip audience, you can afford to be more flashy, more informal and relaxed. Remember too that there is something of a divide between the current 20-somethings and those in their mid-to-late thirties. The 20-somethings and under have used the web a lot when growing up. They're websavvy. Older people, even people in their late thirties, aren't guaranteed to be comfortable with the web so you should try to be conscious of this. It's another reason to limit the flashy stuff on your site if you are catering to an audience that is likely to be quite unfamiliar with the web.

You should definitely make sure your website's content is focused on the primary goal: selling your product and service. Avoid a mishmash of content. A site that has lots of unrelated information is not likely to draw your customer in. At least, it's not likely to draw them in quickly so you'll lose at least a portion of your customers. If your business offers several products, dedicate a page to each one instead of trying to sell them all from one page.

When it comes to website content, you also need to bear in mind that even the most professionally designed website won't sell anything if potential customers don't believe in it. A clear privacy statement is one way to build your credibility and to achieve maximum effect, you should provide a prominent link to your privacy statement from every page on the site and at any location that you are asking your visitors for personal information. Always provide legitimate contact information online.

Another thing to note: navigating your site should be easy because smooth navigation basically enhances convenience for your visitors. Another way to enhance navigation of your site is to add good search and catalog features as very few visitors have the patience to navigate through the whole website to find what they are looking for.

Make sure the content, look, feel, and design of your site are consistent. Studies show that visitors don't like feeling that they have gone from one site to another so try to keep colors and themes constistent.

Make your website interactive and have it in touch with the general feel of your business. Add feedback forms as well as email forms if possible as this will allow your prospective customers to ask you any questions they might have. Larger corporations and online businesses have realized the value of intereacting with clients on a personal level; one-to-one where possible. You should make very effort to listen and respond to your customer so make it possible for them to reach you.

If your website allows for visitor comment and it looks personal and reflective of your business, you're several steps closer to having your visitor's trust. This will increase your sales. You should always try to ensure that your website presents the 'right' image of your company.

Last but definitely not least, you need to make sure that your wesite contains riveting content. Good content sells a business to a customer. Just as every other element of your website is reflective of your business and the company image you want to put out, so too your content should convey a specific message – the right message – about your company.

Have others review, critique and edit your copy to insure it is delivering the intended message. You should try the same thing with your website before it goes live as this will help you avoid any potential probems and it will give you validation if your site is good.

This book will help you to learn various tips and tricks for adding great content and creating and maintaining a dynamic website.

Step Six: You Must Work to Drive Traffic To Your Site
This book will also show you ways to drive traffic to your site and this is a crucial process because, even the best website is not going to secure sales for you if you don't

have any customers. You aren't going to get any customers unless you have plenty of features in place to catch attention.

<u>Step Seven: You Must Monitor and Fine Tune Your Marketing Processes to Ensure Maximum Efficiency and Impact</u>
After implementation, it is important to make frequent reviews to monitor and fine tune the programmes and strategies as the business environment is very dynamic. The good web hosting provider would have c/panel facilities for the web owners to analyse the statistical data pertaining to the number of visitors, which web page is most popular with the visitors, the frequency of visitors etc. Such statistical analysis is useful for one to monitor and further fine tune the website to improve on sales conversion.

Principles to Guide Your Strategy: Consumer Motivation

Consumers and people in general have never been able to understand or appreciate their own motivations. People don't think about them, which is why this part of the mind that does motivate us is referred to as the unconscious. But although consumers do not think about their motives, they do experience them and they do act on them.

Motivation applies not only to consumer behavior, but to all human behavior in any situation. However, since consumers do not actively "think" about their motives, it is difficult to really ask what they are. Given this, traditional market research is not an option for studying consumer emotions. You need to come up with something else.

Furthermore, researchers do not study the role of emotions in everyday life, since emotions are hard to study in a scientific way. Since many researchers have been unable to study emotions directly, they often discredit the whole idea of an unconscious mind and any attempt to describe behavior on anything but the conscious level. Discredited, much of the research on the unconscious mind and motivation as a part of it has been kept underground. Motivation has remained a mystery, despite the reality that advertisers, salespersons, and marketers need to understand motivation to be effective. They especially need to understand the motivation that relates to their products and services so that they can market to the mind. Emotion is the third dimension of marketing.

The five major motivational groups that we have found on the unconscious side are as follows:

1. The Orientation Motives (person, place, time, and circumstances)
2. The Survival Motives (spiritual, physical, sexual, and territorial)
3. The Adaptation Motive
4. The Expectation Motive
5. The Play Motive

1. The Orientation Motives

Everyone needs to remain oriented to their external reality and has a mechanism within themselves that keeps them oriented, rather like the internal compass mechanism that keeps a migratory bird on course.

There are four motivational subgroups within the Orientation Motives:

- Orientation to person
- Orientation to place
- Orientation to time
- Orientation to circumstances

2. Survival Motives

The Survival Motives are the strongest of all the motives. Like the Orientation Motives, they go unnoticed in the unconscious mind unless it is some threat by an external force. There are four motivational subgroups within the survival group, presented in order of importance from strongest to weakest:

- Spiritual survival (psychological)
- Physical survival
- Territorial survival
- Sexual survival

3. Adaptation Motive

We all have a strong motive to adapt to our climate, culture, group, beliefs, and surroundings. If smoking cigarettes is trendy, then people will smoke, regardless of how it effects their physical survival and their health. This motive may be stronger than the Physical Survival Motive, since people will do things that are unwise in terms of their physical survival for adaptation. Cigarette smoking is one obvious example. Another is the use of recreational drugs that present serious health risks, like cocaine. Adaptation is the most well established of all the motives. It is even seen in neonates in utero on diagnostic ultrasounds as they move their hands to their faces in an effort to adapt to that environment. Infants continue this behavior during the first six to seven months of life. In adolescence and adulthood adaptation takes on the form of imitation as well.

4. Expectation Motive

The Expectation Motive relates to hope and trust and the way that people view the future. We all have an innate faith and belief that the future will work itself out in a positive way. It's not false optimism or idealism, but simply a trust that one day will follow the other; it's really nothing more than a way to deal with the future.

5. Play Motive
Yes, we are all motivated to have fun.

When it comes to a successful marketing campaign, you should always look to tap into these motivations.

Motivations and Marketing

Motives, like spiritual survival, physical survival, etc., are abstractions. And consumers do not respond to abstractions. Extensive research shows that pictures are retained better than concrete words and concrete words are retained better than abstract words.

Coty and Calvin Klein once attempted to design motives into their advertising by talking about the spiritual side of women. This was believed to be a unique approach but, for most people the word "spiritual" is an abstraction; if it means anything, it's something about religion and not something to do with psychology, as is the case in advertising. In advertising, it is a psychological construct that is present in the mind. Effective advertising needs to address this in a way that is not abstract.

Did the advertising by Coty and Calvin Klein work? It may have. But it would be stronger if they addressed the elements of spiritual survival rather than just the motive as an abstract. Another problem with their approach: spiritual survival may not be the strongest motivation determining a woman's use of cosmetics. In cosmetics, orientation to person is found by researchers to be more influential and persuasive.

The design of effective motivational advertising, then, should be in the appeal to the elements of the motives rather than to the motives directly. Put another way, a beautiful sunset is something everyone can see and appreciate; try and describe the beauty and the image is distorted by the detail of the description.

For example, in talking about food, most food marketers agree that close-up color pictures of the food product itself are a very effective way to market and advertise certain food products. It makes more sense to picture the food itself than to talk about physical survival. Physical survival, although easy to understand, is an abstraction but anyone can relate to the picture of a hamburger or a cheeseburger with fries!

Look at what happens when advertisers approach sexual survival as a motive. One example was Brooke Shields in Calvin Klein jeans. The result: many people were offended; again in 1995 so many people were offended by the new round ads that the Calvin Klein company was obliged to pull the ads and a federal investigation ensued. The lesson to learn from this: sexual survival can be highly controversial and thus spiritual survival is assaulted and offended.

When it comes to using spiritual motives in advertisng, most people understand what it means to be renewed, refreshed. These are the finer points of motivation and there are very few who cannot understand them. Motives should never be directly addressed. Focus instead on the elements of the motives and in scenarios that address these elements.

Motivational Advertising Should Be Layered
If there is already a logical reason that a consumer would like to buy your product, two layers of emotion are generally enough. Beyond that, consumers begin to get confused and disoriented, which leads to a fast turnoff. Avoid clutter.

Direct Penetration of the Unconscious with Personalizations
Advertising that is directed toward the motivational structures is the type of advertising that people will personalize. Personalization leads to recall. People will recall what they can personalize.

Ads that penetrate the unconscious are more enduring, even if they are not liked by the consumer. Personalizations must be product related, motivational, and emotional. When they meet these three criteria, recall is assured.

Positive and Negative Suggestions
There is no logic in the unconscious mind; it receives all suggestions as undirectional. Consider Mr. Whipple telling shoppers, "Please don't squeeze the Charmin!" Telling shoppers not to pick up the Charmin was found to be an extremely successful way of getting them to do just the opposite.

Absurdities
Absurdities are mnemonics. By definition they increase recall and although they are not as motivating as personalizations, but they are memorable. Absurdities have the advantage of being memorable, but they are not necessarily motivating or personal..

Designing Successful Marketing Campaigns
To get an idea of what constitutes a successful advertising campaign, look at the successful advertising campaigns run by major companies in the past. Take Avis, with their Number Two campaign. The positioning of this campaign was perfect: Avis said, "We're number two," and in saying so, they positioned themselves against the leader in the rental car market. Avis went one step further and said, "and we try harder"; a motivational statement that speaks directly to orientation to circumstances. "We're number two and we try harder." The first part is a positioning statement, the second part, a motivational statement.

One of the most memorable advertising campaigns ever run was the 1982-83 Coke series that used "Mean" Joe Greene of the Pittsburgh Steelers as a spokesperson. It was memorable because it was highly motivational. The television ad had Joe Greene, worn out from a game and on his way to the locker room, stop to talk with a small boy who offers him a Coke. The boy could not have been more than eight and so this commercial grabbed the hearts of Americans. It is strong and persuasive; commercials like this are almost always targeted to the spiritual survival level. The element involved here is affirming acceptance. Joe Greene was like a god for youngsters and sports fans. In the ad, he bends down to an eight year old when he is offered a Coke. The star takes the Coke and all Americans who watch feel just what that boy felt: the power of affirming acceptance by a major player on the American sports scene; spiritual survival in motivation.

For another example we can look to McDonald's. In the early days, they marketed to the level of physical survival. "To all beef patties, special sauce, lettuce, cheese, pickles, onions on a sesame seed bun!" This slogan caught on because it deals with food, one of the major elements of the Physical Survival Motive.

When McDonald's elevated its advertising to the next level of motivation, the slogan changed. "You deserve a break today" establishes circumstances. From this it moved on to family values and spiritual survival, which was as high as it could go on the motivational hierarchy.

Wendy's, Burger King, and the others have stayed with food, which is the major element of what they sell, on the physical survival level. Perhaps not the strongest advertising, but it is safe. As Wendy's Dave Thomas says, "When you gotta have one, you gotta have one." The food is the element and physical survival the motive. However, Wendy's also uses Dave Thomas, the founder, and many people are aware that he does not even have a high school diploma! This adds another major motivation: expectation.

Now that we've looked at winning marketing strategies for businesses, it's time to take a look at the type of business venture that most needs a winning strategy…that is, businesses struggling to make ends meet…businesses in need of turnaround.

Chapter 2: Business Turnaround

"The world will stand apart for the man who knows where he is going"
Swami Vivekananda

Introduction
An ailing business needs a new angle, a fresh approach. It also needs stabilization, to regain control over its current state; stop the heamorraging of money and resources that is the common result of bad business.

Not surprisingly, perhaps, to most individuals with business acumen, the internet is an excellent resource, not only for business in general, but for business turnaround in particular.

The Internet is nothing short of revolutionary in the way that it opens up a global market for businesses. Yes, a global market. If you haven't got a website, if you know nothing about what your website can do to promote your business, then it's time to start taking notes and rethinking your business approach, particularly if your company is currently in trouble. Internet marketing strategies can certainly revive the fortunes of down-and-out companies. The process starts here, with consumers and the internet.

The Internet Today
"There are certain moments when you can see the future with such clarity it nearly takes your breath away"; so begins one of severeal million articles on the internet and the way it has changed the world. Is it a cliché to call the internet a window into the future; an indication of how people will communicate and interact? Will everything take place online someday? Certainly the internet is changing the way the world works and it's beginning by churning up the global market economy...

India, for example, a nation of one billion people, despite enormous challenges, is on the verge of something spectacular. Out of poverty emerges a great new force in high-tech competition. A company called Wipro Ltd is bringing new life to the region and investing massive amounts of funds in development.

When they caught media attention in India, personnel of Wirpo Ltd were working on a project for a company based eleven and a half time zones away, in Nashville, Tennessee. CNA Life called on Wirpo's expertise to bring about to reengineer its business processes and the improvement of their performance. Wipro employees set the strategy, then designed and architected the system. It's high-level stuff, a "mission critical" application.

Amazingly, a decade ago, Wipro was selling cooking oil and personal computers, mostly in India, barely making a profit and certainly staying below the radar. Today, it is worth a staggering $903 million per year and it's opperating on a global market, with most of its business now coming from information-technology services.

Since 1997, Wipro's revenue has grown by an average of 26% per year. Profits have grown by 69% and its 15,000 technologists write software, integrate back-office solutions, design semiconductors, debug applications, take orders, and field help calls for some of the biggest companies in the world.

Wipro is as good as any of its competitors around the world. Better perhaps, maybe because they are cheaper. Wipro is, on average about 40% cheaper than its competitors, including comparable American companies.

Three years ago, Bangalore was called the software world's biggest body shop. Now Wipro and a few of their competitors are graduating. Wipro is now competing with Accenture, EDS, IBM, and the big accounting firms. It's winning, too.

Whether you consider these developments as positives or negatives depends on your world view and general understanding of a whole host of matters. In Bangalore, Wipro's growth carries tremendous national significance. In America, where technology-services companies struggle with weak stock prices and uncertain growth prospects, the rise of a tough, low-cost competitor causes some serious concerns.

Ganesh Narasimhaiya (his business card reads simply Ganesh N.) is thirty years old, enjoys cricket, R&B music, bowling, and he lives with his parents in Bangalore. He earned a bachelor's degree in electronics and communications, and he can spit out code in a variety of languages: COBOL, Java, UML (Unified Modeling Language) and the like.

In the past three years, Ganesh has worked on high-level projects for Wipro all over the world. He has helped GE Medical Systems establish a logistics application throughout Southeast Asia. He proposed a plan to consolidate and synchronize security solutions across a British client's e-business applications.

"I want to be on the cutting edge of technology," says Ganesh. He's smart and ambitious; dedicated and prepared to work eighteen or nineteen hours a day at a customer site.

Ganesh is part of Wipro's edge. The company is building a force of high-level strategists, increasingly focused on specific industries. With Ganesh and his coworkers firing away at their work, Wipro can play the ace up their sleeve: offshore outsourcing solutions that dramatically lower clients' expenses.

The American information economy has made the country somewhat complacent; comfortable with a competitive advantage of knowledge and innovation. Companies based in the US have justified charging premium prices because the country has the best-trained talent delivering top-quality information solutions the world over. When the bulk of manufacturing jobs went overseas in the 1980s concern was relatively short-lived; the US remained the world-leader in innovative thinking and so-called "white-collar brain work". But what if brain work can be done anywhere? What if it can be done for less outside of the United States?

If technology companies could work anywhere, the significance and scope of Wipro would be seriously underminded. The company has certainly understood the hardest lesson of the global economy: that peddling a low-cost service can't lead to sustainable growth and profitability. If what you do can be done by anyone, someone will always be happy to do it for less.

Wipro has also understood the importance of developing long-term relationships with clients, rather than having short-term relationships to service specific needs. After hiring out technical workers on-demand in the 1990s, today, in Electornic City, Wipro has development centers dedicated to meet the needs of Hewlett-Packard, GM, and dozens of other major global companies. Weyerhaeuser, a lumber company, has centers in Bangalore, Chennai, and the United States; one in each of these locations, housing, in total, more than two hundred engineers. The relationship with Wipro began in 1999 with two Wipro employees undertaking a modest on-site analysis at Weyerhaeuser's headquarters in the US. Wipro now develops, maintains, and supports a broad array of Weyerhaeuser applications from the Wipro base in Bangalore.

What Wipro puts first, however, is quality. In six years, the company has trained over seven thousand employees in Six Sigma and completed over a thousand projects. Six years ago, Fast Company profiled a team at Lockheed-Martin that wrote nearly perfect code ("They Write the Right Stuff," Dec: Jan 1997). The team's claim to fame: It was one of only four outfits in the world to achieve Level 5 certification from the Software Engineering Institute. Wipro has Level 5 certification in three different categories. It's eye-glazing stuff and an amazing achievement.

The impressive achievement of the Wipro company are probably a fairly good indicator of what's to come in areas of the world that are currently overlooked by most of the rest of the developed world. The reality is, however, that the internet is allowing companies to get ahead, to turn their businesses around, and really become trailblazers of the new world economy.

How do companies like Wipro come to enjoy the limelight of center stage? In the beginning, there was the Internet. It worked – at least, people could use it. More to the point, it was misunderstood as a resource by just about everyone.

What About Business Turn-Around and the Internet?

It's fairly clear that the internet has a great deal to contribute to the turnaround process; there are several hundred books on the subject on internet marketing and corporate turnaround. by now and probably plenty more to come.

Most of the books on internet marketing do not cover in depth on how it can be used to turnaround the fortunes of companies. The majority of corporate turnaround books are written by executives who have turned around Fortune 500 companies. In achieving turnaround, the vast majority of these authors have been able to cut large numbers of employees, tap pension funds, and tap bank funds to raise cash and decrease debt. Most of the time, implementing a turnaround, the Fortune 500 companies also have large stocks of assets and other funding sources they can use to rebuild the company.

Although it is always impressive to implement a turnaround and be a success, even with the advantage of considerable resources, very few small to midsized companies have notable resources at their disposal to assist the process. Most small businesses can have a tough time acquiring a line of credit and most don't have assets to sell. Increasing the company's cash position is very difficult; what is required doesn't remotely resemble the process, and can't afford to lay off large numbers of people.

Another bundle of books for business turnaround focus on financial and accounting issues. Unfortunately, many of these books are also of very limited use to small business owners. The majority deal only with half of the problem faced by an executive in a turnaround. None of them explain how to write business plans to raise new capital or how to develop marketing and sales plans to increase sales. They also avoid discussion of the people management issues and the common mistakes the leaders make.

Starting and turning around small to medium sized companies offers both unique and sometimes very painful challenges. To accomplish corporate turnarounds successfully you need a great deal of energy, self-confidence, resiliency, and positive mental attitude. Your employees, shareholders, and family will all be looking to you for leadership and stability.

Business leaders who find themselves in a turnaround situation are initially afraid and likely to question whether they are qualified to fix their company. They often feel worthless and very much isolated by the pressures of a failing business. Unfortunately, those feelings can't be allowed to last long or failure will indeed be imminent.

There are several steps to turning a business around: recognizing that your company needs to be fixed and determining how to fix it while maintaining control. Before embarking on this process, which nowadays should rely quite heavily on the internet and technology, it is helpful to review some information on business bankruptcies and failures published in a 1997 Small Business Administration (SBA) report.

According to the SBA, the failure rate of small business in the United States rose by 16.6 percent between 1986 and 1996. Business bankruptcies also increased by 5.3 percent in 1996, rising from 50,516 in 1995 to 53,214 in 1996.

If your business really is in trouble, these figures should really convince you: you are not alone.

Of course, if your company is in trouble, it's likely that you didn't find yourself in this state overnight. Most companies find that their business flounders over a period of a few months or years.

So what are the most common symptoms exhibited by a company in trouble? This list should give you some idea of what you're up against.

- Sales decrease while the general market is seen to grow
- Current customers are leaving for reasons that you can't control
- Clients complain their calls aren't being returned
- Most client projects run over their budget
- Profits are declining while expenses are rising
- Employees are telling each other and customers, they aren't sure of the company's direction
- Employees are telling management there's no meaningful leadership
- Employees are arriving late and leaving early
- Employee monthly meetings have stopped
- Good employees are leaving the company
- Employees have stopped trusting management
- Employees are bickering over minute details
- Weekly management meetings have been set aside
- Management isn't working as a team
- The company can't afford to pay taxes
- The company is falling behind paying its vendors

To turn your ailing business around, you need to implement a ten key phase to achieve a successful turnaround for your small to medium-size business.

The steps you need are as follows:

The General Plan For A Turnaround

1. Write business plan, a sales and marketing plan, and an operation plan
You need to establish the future of your company. Your business plan should establish your overall objectives, your planned structure, your long and short term goals, you marketing and sales strategies, and your plans for implementation. Your sales and marketing plans should focus on these areas includes in your business plan and provide more detail for both areas.

2. Unify your team by meeting with key personnel to discuss the plans
Before you finalize your three plans (business, sales and marketing, and operation), you need to have an informal but detailed discussion with all the key members of your company's team. The purpose of this meeting is to get their input and ideas about the business; where it should be going and how it is going to get there. You also need to thoroughly review the plan, and make notes of what your team members have to say.

3. Weigh the advice of your key personnel and look to revise your plans
After you undertake a comprehensive review of your plan, facilitating the ideas and opinions of your key personnel, you should revise the plan. The revised version should be

distributed to your key executives so they can sign off on it or voice additional concerns. When the plan is ready and approved, you should make a formal presentation to your board of directors and employees.

4. Arrange a formal company meeting to present your plan of action
Be prepared to hand each of your employee a copy of your business plan, marketing and sales plan, and operation plan. The purpose of your company meeting is to formally recognize the problem with your business with your employees and discuss your plans to fix it. When you present your formal plans, be prepared to take questions. Indeed, you should actively encourage open discussion with your employees to take suggestions and note concerns.

5. Meet with customers
Even if you have a very small customer base, ensure that every one knows what you're planning for the business. Be open and honest about the situation; clear and concise about your plans. If your company has been in trouble for some time, be prepared to address rumors – at least, the effects of rumors – that have circulated the business community. Some of your key customers may have becoming nervous and some may even have looked for new vendors. You're objective is to reassure your customers while being totally truthful.

6. Meet with vendors
Company vendors get nervous when they hear one of their customers is struggling; you'll probably be surprised by how fast news travels. It's likely that most of your vendors will be aware that you're having trouble. That said, you should still endeavor to give a formal explanation of the situation and, more particularly, of your plans for turnaround. Set everyone at ease.

7. Contact tax authorities
If part of your business issue is that you are short of money, it's unlikely you can pay your local, county, state, and federal taxes. If this is the case, the proper course of action is to contact the tax authorities and explain the situation. You'll find them much more receptive to you if you are do this rather than appear to be dodging your obligations.

8. Get in touch with your bank
If you have one or more loans or lines of credit, call your loan officers and tell them you need to meet in person. When you meet,to discuss the problem, be clear about your plan of action and appear confident about the proposed solutions.

9. Cut your losses
Nobody likes to cut back resources and nobody likes to let go of employees but it is necessary when your business is in trouble. You need to downsize. First, make a list of all your business expenses and see what you can elminiate from your weekly, monthly, and annual bills. Consider this: you need to buy time. Also you should keep only the employees who are essential to your business. You should keep only those who bring in, make, and service sales.

10. Use the Internet to your advantage

Review your company's current use of the internet as a resource. Read through this guide, determine what internet-based resources are good for your business. Make a plan for the implementation of your program and away you go.

Turning a business around using the internet as a primary tool is challenging but exciting. There are many different tools that you can use to promote your business. The principle tool is your website but there are many secondary tools that can help you make the most of having a live site, everything from company blogs to video feeds, from banner exchange advertising to pay per click programs.

In the last decade or so, Internet expanded into a huge market, accessible to companies all over the world. Some of the biggest companies in the world have taken advantage of the Internet to achieve their status, making the most of low-cost advertising and electronic commerce, commonly known as e-commerce. The Internet is the fastest way to spread information and it allows you to spread information to a vast, seemingly limitless number of people. It has also revolutionized shopping and marketing by allowing a company to market a product to a specific person and a specific group of people.

Personalized marketing using MySpace and Friendster allows thousands of Internet users advertise and make friends online. Many of these users are teens and adolescents. The most common age group is defined as 13 to 25 years olds. Thanks to social networking – this is the name given to programs like MySpace and Friendster – individuals and businesses have a wealth of information about individual users that helps to determine what they will purchase online.

A very ineffective way of advertising on the internet is using spam emails. Most email providers offer protection against email spam. Most spam messages are sent automatically to everybody in the email database of the company or person that is spamming.

Adware is another very ineffective way of advertising as most people simply close a popup window when it shows up, not bothering to read it, or they have popup blockers as part of their internet security.

If you want to turn your company around using the internet, the best approach is to use a number of different methods to advertise and promote your business, matching the effectiveness of the various methods to your specific requirements and the limitations of your budget.

Rebuilding Morale

One of the key elements of your turnaround will be the rebuilding of your company's morale, targeting the highest and the lowest levels of your company. If your company is in trouble, it's likely that your employees, from your management level exectutives right on down to your guys on the front line, will all be feeling the stress and strain of the situation. If they're heavily invested in the company on an emotional level, then they are probably feeling that they are in part responsible. They're probably losing confidence in themselves and, in the long run, they're looking at themselves as failures.

Business Turnaround: Adjusting Moral

This is what happens in organizations that are mismanaged. People doubt themselves and those around them. Being a part of the organization no longer makes them feel good; instead of getting in early and staying late, people start to show up late and look for excuses to leave early. They want to be at the office for the bare minimum time required to cash in a paycheck. And the negativity spread doesn't stop there. Friends of employees, relatives who were interested in joining the organization or perhaps generating some business; they are told to stay away. The company becomes, in the eyes of everyone around it, the next Titanic, doomed to sink and sink quickly.

The following steps should help you address the problem of poor morale, but remember, this should be an ongoing process. Even while you are implementing some of the ideas put forward in this book to revamp your company with a dynamic online presence, you should

1. Hold a company-wide meeting to single out various employees for their successes. This will help to demonstrate to your work force that successful people are a part of their team.

2. Set aside time to talk about how management and employees are going to fix the company's problems together. Admit to past mistakes made by management. People join small companies because they like to know they are having an impact, that what they say and how they feel matters. Make sure your employees feel that they are having an impact. As a turnaround CEO, you are encouraged to start a blog for the staff and customers to address any common anxieties and worries pertaining to the future of the company.

3. Meet with each employee individually to find out what they think needs to be done to get the company back on track. Ask specifically how management can help them with their job.

4. Send notices about new sales and post compliments received from clients. This allows employees to feel proud of their accomplishments and avoids management having to tell every individual what a good job they are doing.

5. Familiarize yourself with your employees' strengths and weaknesses. Use your knowledge to set them up to succeed. All too often management gives employees directives that are beyond their abilities. Don't make this mistake or your employees will feel like they're drowning in failure.

6. Compliment employees for their work in front of their clients when possible. Nothing makes an employee feel better or more valuable than being complimented by their boss in front of a client.

7. Promote from within your company ranks. Nothing demonstrates the quality of talent better than promoting existing employees. It makes a statement that management believes the talent already exists within the organization. Your employees will feel they have better job security and better opportunities at your company than they might have somewhere else. This is an important feeling to foster.

8. When possible, let go of people who aren't pulling their weight and those who aren't team players. If your employees see that someone can get away with doing a slack job, your authority will be undermined. Avoid this if possible, especially when you're looking to rebuild moral.

9. Let employees know when management has taken and implemented a suggestion scheme to solicit feedback from the ranks. Show that management values employee input.

10. Encourage risk and reward innovation. If the risk taker makes a mistake, remind them of all the chances other managers took that failed. Tell them that if management didn't have confidence in their judgment, they wouldn't have let them take the risk at all.

Rebuilding morale takes time and patience. People don't lose their confidence overnight. It slowly erodes.

Business Turnaround: Getting A Loan
There are three essential components to a successful loan application; three things that your bank will look for in your application. The Three "c's" are character, credit and collateral.

Character means the bank is confident in you. It's about not having a criminal record, but it's also about giving your banker the confidence that you're not going to suddenly disappear if the business gets in trouble. When it comes to establishing character, you should demonstrate the community such as long residence, family ties, and home ownership.

You should also have a clean credit history. And while bankers like good character and good credit, but they live for solid collateral such as equipment, buildings, and trucks. Inventory, raw material and goods are second choices. These lose value more quickly than fixed assets but they are still quite valuable.

Before you settle on a bank, a loan type, and any sort of terms, you should check the criteria for business loans. These critera vary much more widely than criteria for consumer loans and often varies quite a bit from one banker to the next, even the same bank.

There's some general information you should take into consideration:
- New business usually have a financial risk
- Fixed assets such as machinery or buildings can almost always be financed
- Current assets such as inventory or goods can increase your loan chances
- 2+ years of profitable operation greatly increases your loan chances
- The larger the owner's investment in the business the better your chances of getting a loan
- To get a loan for your small corporation, a shareholder will often have to provide a personal guarantee
- It is difficult to get loans to offset operating losses
- It is usually possible to get a loan to modestly expand a profitable business

An important question: can you still get money when the bank declines your initial loan application? The answer is, generally yes. If your bank has declined your business loan application, you might have more lucky applying as an individual. Banks are much more lenient when lending to consumers instead of businesses. You may be able to borrow money from the bank as a consumer and then personally invest the funds in your business. You should be honest about your intentions – the purpose of the loan – but it's likely that, if you were denied a business loan, you'll still be awarded a consumer loan, particularly if you have collateral. A home equity loan, for example, can be invested in your business. The bank feels safer lending to you under these circumstances because their statistics show that home equity loans are much more likely to be repaid than loans for brand new businesses. Car loans are another good option.

Generally, you should try to observe basic etiquette when you go to the bank to apply for a loan. You should definitely go in person. But don't just show up. You should call ahead to make an appointment and ask the receptionist if you can make an appointment with the person who can handle your consumer loan application. If possible, it is helpful to have a referral from someone.Don't just show up in person--first make an appointment by phone. Ask the receptionist in the bank or the loan department for the name of the appropriate person who would handle your loan request. Of course it would be better to get a referral from a friend or advisor such as your lawyer or accountant to a loan officer at the bank. Regardless of how it plays out, when you get the name of the appropriate loan officer ask for an appointment and don't offer any more details over the phone, unless the loan officer requests them. Keep in mind the general rule: the more details you offer over the phone, the greater the chance you won't get the appointment.

Your objective when making the appointment and during the appointment is to sound matter of fact, confident, and, above all, not in need of money. This will make you seem like the person the bank wants to lend to.

Business Turnaround: Summary

For the most part, business turnaround is about planning. It involves identifying the problem areas and the positive areas; reducing the problems and accentuating the positive elements of your business.

Planning is also the most basic element of internet marketing success and it will make all the difference as you work to turn your business around using the internet as your chief resource.

Chapter 3: Internet and Business Turnaround

Why do you want a website?
Try answering this question for yourself. Why does your company want to have a website?

Your answer may be one of the following:

1. It looks good to have a website address on the business card
2. Dot com is everywhere and having a website would make me a part of the revolution
3. Internet is a great marketing tool and I would like to use it to my advantage

You are not wrong if you have chosen 1 or 2 or both, but you are certainly aware of what Internet can do for you and are looking for how to do it if you choose 3.

True, having a website must be preceded with a clear understanding of why you should have a website.

A website typically can be used to:

1. Reach Out
You may want to use your website as a medium to reach out to customers from all geographic areas and make your business known in far off territories. This can help you get prospects you'd never have reached otherwise.

2. Dispurse Information
You may want to use your website as a permanent billboard for anybody to see and get information about your company, its products and services,

3. Sell Your Products and Services
You may want your website to actually sell your products over the Internet. You may want to use Ecommerce tools so you can receive payments online via credit card from customers all over the world. You can then ship them the goods they want.

Although a website can serve many different purposes, you have to identify your website's core purpose, i.e to generate leads, support your traditional marketing, or establish a virtual shopping store. Having a clear purpose in mind will focus your efforts to develop your website. A clearly defined purpose will add strength to your Internet marketing efforts, enhancing your website's success.

You are expected to have a website
Well, websites are useful but there's another very important reason to have one for your business – in this day and age, you are expected to have one!

With the Internet penetrating into every community in the world you're expected to have a website accessible to both web surfers and established prospects looking to find out more about your business, your products, and services.

The following functions of the website will help you establish and further define your purpose.

1. **Position yourself to be found where customers are searching** - You are at a serious disadvantage if you don't exist in the database of search engines and aren't anywhere in the search engine results. Key word optimization and meta tagging are essential for the success of your website. Don't overlook this technique and invest in professional web-design and search engine optimization help if you need.

2. **Sell more** - To create more customers you need to tell people you exist. To make greater profits you need more customers and Internet is one great tool to reach out to people at minimum cost – so why not try it out

3. **Make it more convenient for your buyers** – It is cost effective, fast, and simple for prospective customers to visit your website instead of driving to your physical location. If your business can serve long-distance clients, those who are not within an easy distance of your company's physical location, then you also expand your market of potential customers.

4. **Beat the competition** – Your customer is loaded with choices. Your competitors are doing all they can to get their attention. Even though a customer may be interested in your business, it's easy for them to choose another company over you if reaching out to you proves to be inconvenient in any way.

5. **Improve your advertising efficiency** – You've spent hundreds of dollars advertising your business; in newspapers, magazines, radio or T.V. You understand the importance of being visible to customers but you'd certainly like to cut your costs. Start exploring your Internet-based marketing options, improving your leads and sales conversions while also cutting back on costs.

6. **Put your business on autopilot for 24 hours** – It is very important that the customer should be able to reach you when they want to. Having a website is like having any other building or a storefront. On the web you can be available anytime, taking advantage of various technologies to make information about your products and services around the clock This has a clear advantage over traditional advertising methods – newspapers, magazines, flyers etc as the life span of your advertisement is virtually unlimited. A website means constant presence.

7. **Cut costs while expanding your influence** – In traditional business strategies, expansion involves opening up new offices in various cities. This is how

businesses traditionally secured a wider customer base; limited by geography. Opening offices in various cities is an expensive preposition. Not only do you need to invest in real estate, you incur huge overheads with manpower, maintenance, and communication costs for each establishment. With a website your business has no physical restrictions; it can be accessed by potential customers anywhere in the world. You don't need multiple office locations just to reach your customers and, if you decide to centralize your operations, you may find you're improving efficiency and cuts costs drastically.

8. **One world; one address** – Ever noticed how jumbled marketing material looks when you have five or six physical addresses, three or four telephone numbers, and a couple of fax lines? Well, online businesses need only advertise one address: yourname@yourcompany.com! Stylish – isn't it!

9. **It business@light.speed** – Imagine you're a customer searching for information over the net. You come across a business website. You can request a service or product quote via e-mail. How about receiving the quote in your mailbox in 10 minutes! Fantastic isn't it? In today's world speed is important and with a website you are free to conduct your business at a lightning speed.

10. **No more Chinese Whispers!** – Since all your visitors from all over the world will see the same information on your website, there is no chance of your message getting diluted or mismashed. Everyone reads your message, as you wrote it.

11. **Say goodbye to the Right Location** – A website is your location. It doesn't get much better; what with cheap rent and great amenities. And building the perfect website is a lot cheaper than renovating an office space! The better your website, the better the impression you ensure that customers are interested in the quality of your products and the service they get. When you operate online, they don't need to be preoccupied about your location.

12. **Help democratizes the business world** – Everyone can have a great website. Small businesses are equal to the giants in the online world. On the web, no customer is concerned about the size of your office.

13. **Update easily:** Having a website makes it really simple to add, modify, edit, and delete content – or simply update info on latest products or services at almost no cost at all and that too in a matter of few minutes.

14. **Foster two-way communication** – You can request feedback from your clients or start a message board so your customers can discuss their experiences with your products.

15. **Provide customer service online** – A website makes it possible to provide customer service quickly and efficiently. Tell your customers about new product features, how to use your products, and how to troubleshoot most problems. You

can also have a help center for your customers to login and resolve small troubles with the product all by themselves. For complex queries, if your company staff is large enough, you can have live chat to problems in real time. This helps build credibility and reputation on the website.

To sell products to customers anywhere in the world, it is critical for businesses to have an excellent, functional, dynamic website.

Having a website will give teeth to your basic Internet marketing efforts. For other advanced techniques, a website is your basic requirement to make a splash in the virtual world.

Having your own professional website for free!
Gone are the days when you needed the help of an expert (and expensive) web designer. There are several softwares, which contain preprogrammed templates that you can use; www.moonfruit.com is one such portal. The portal offers various website templates, including "Business", which you can choose to make a business site. There are a host of other widgets like clocks and counters, images, photo gallery, message board, and a whole lot of other features depending on whether you use the portal for free or upgrade as a paid user. For members who choose to pay, there are seller features that help you incorporate Ecommerce features, like a shopping cart and arrangement for receiving money as well. You can add music and video to your website as well.

In short, you can have a very professional looking, neat, impressive, and fully functional website in a matter of minutes. You would know it after exploring Moonfruit.

There are various other portals like www.moonfruit.com offering web hosting. Check it out and have your presence on the net right now!

Qualities of a good website
A good site is one that brings web traffic – lots of it! Your company website must get targeted traffic and must convince them to act according to your purpose. The following factors will help you align your website towards getting more eyeballs.

Choice of URL

URL or the "Universal Resource Locator" should match your business and if possible tell a word or two about your business. It should have the keywords associated with your business and must be easy to spell and remember. You may want to check whether the URL you are planning to have is available or not. Godaddy.com lets you know the availability of a particular name along with its domain (.com, .net, .biz etc). In case the URL you desperately want is already taken you can visit whois.com to have the contact details of the owner and try persuading him to sell it to you. It can however be an expensive preposition. You may try to get creative with your site name and try combining two or three words relevant to your business.

URLs can be registered for a minimum of one year. You need to renew your registration after the end of the period you have paid for.

Registering a URL typically comes with following services:

- ✓ Free email account
- ✓ Free URL forwarding
- ✓ Free domain locking; etc

*tiny URL
Hosting your website

Most of the people think that websites exist on the web. This web, however, is a network of computers. The content of your website is stored in a computer from where it can be accessed by Internet users. The computers used are special; they are called "servers". You need to pay to have your content on a server. A preliminary search at google.com would bring up various web hosting companies. However, you may look out for the following parameters before closing in:

1. Money: Compare the offers of various web-hosting companies. There can be huge differences.
2. Storage Space: Ensure that your web hosting company can give you enough space for your needs. What if there is a sudden surge of traffic to your site? Can your web hosting company take care of that – check it out
3. Technical Support: You need your website to be up all the time. You may want to verify the track record of the company in providing good backend support.
4. Security: Your web hosting company must have sufficient security arrangement in place so that your website is not hacked.
5. Other features: Various web hosting companies would have various free or promotional offers for you. Check out who is giving out the best package.

Website Design
Creative Aspects

It's very much like the adage: "First Impression is the last impression". On the first note your website must look good and must feel in line with the message you want to convey. The graphics, font, pictures, arrangement of text should be well organized and of a high quality. It should be pleasing, inviting, inspiring trustworthy, developing credibility all at the same time. Challenging isn't it – and this makes the choice of the right web designer all the more critical.

Website design should also help make the navigation within the site an easy affair.

Functional Aspects

Speed Speed Speed!

Patience is something that a typical Internet user does not have. If your site does not show signs of loading within first 5 to 6 seconds, the users starts getting restless and might stray away. Limit using flashy icons and text effects all over your site. They not only distract but also slow down the loading of your site.

No matter how beautiful your website design, if it does not load within 15 to 20 seconds chances are your potential customer will surf away. Site designs should not be heavy. Use of graphics and pictures must be judicious as they tend to slow down the loading.

Content

A surfer attracted to your site may get hugely disappointed if your content does not match up to the promise of your initial design. Great content is what will ultimately convert a potential customer into an actual customer. When a surfer visits your site, they should receive an overview of your company. You must now be able to use the "moment of truth" to your advantage and take it as an opportunity to establish, trust, competence, and credibility.

Your website must be written for your target audience. The content must satisfy the needs of your target audience. Moreover, it must be compelling enough for the user to act in accordance with your purpose (to generate lead, inform, or sell).

Choice of fonts and colors

The content of your site must be readable. Font size and style should be adequate. The color combination must not make the site difficult to read. The safest way is to put black text on a white background. It is easy on eyes.

Page Size

The page should not be too long, but you may be tempted to keep page size short to allow the content to run into several pages. Beware you may annoy visitors to your site if they have page after page to go through. They may lose interest halfway.

Keeping content updated

You must also ensure that your site has fresh content. Renewing your content regularly helps keep the interest alive. You may want to have an event section where you have regular updates. You can have a message board or a blog where users are allowed to post new messages. This keeps the content interesting and promotes interaction. Nothing is more dissatisfying than to visit the homepage of a site that lists an event as upcoming dating back six months!

Navigation

Convenience is what the user is looking at. Make your site easy to review and you win.

Poor site navigation includes dead hyperlinks, links to pages with no links, hidden links, and similar. It is a good idea to have links within the site, so that no matter where the visitor is he can always find a way back to your home page.

Your Website and the Internet

There is no point in having a website if you don't direct traffic to it. You have to work to increase website traffic once you establish an online presence. Even if you've had your website professionally designed and you are selling a great product or service, new potential cients won't find you online unless you're actively promoting your site; unless you actively work to get high traffic and unique visitors. Sitting back and waiting for it to happen won't work.

To increase website traffic you'll have to achieve several key goals.

Ranking high in the major search engines, developing links to a number of relevant sites that can lead to your site, and developing recognition of your company's expertise are your primary goals. Three goals sound fairly straightforward but that's before you think about the number of individuals and businesses that are competing for visitors on the web.

Top spots on the major search engines – Google, Yahoo, MSN, Ask, etc. – are extremely tough to get. Submitting your site will achieve next to nothing; major companies with major budgets pay to have their site submitted every single day to keep top placements. Your website should have keyword rich Meta tags, page titles, and information that will be recognized by the search engines when people are looking for information on your types of products and services. You should also try to think outside of the box to bring attention to your site.

For the best search engine results, each page of your site should focus on a topic of interest. You should use only a couple of keywords, just one or two at a time, focusing on one or two keyword and phrase per page. If you use too many key words in a row, your search engine ranking will drop.

Links are a great, cheap way to promote your site. The basic idea is that you put links to other sites on your site and then have other sites place links back to your site. This should help to increase your website traffic but the key to success is selective linking. You need to link to sites that are relevant to the service or product you provide. Relevance is the key and it will bring you great leads. Your links don't have to be huge banner ads. It's the links that are important.

Another thing to think about: content. Article writing for sites like Ezine.com is increasingly popular. If you're a business owner, you're an expert in at least one area so you should write a couple of short, keyword driven articles to draw attention to you and your company. Submitting articles to surfing webs, forums, and online clubs will get your name and your company's name in the limelight. In author profile sections you can include a link to your website. Ideally, your articles should include linking text that will take readers to different pages on your website. These can generate traffic to very specific products or services if placed correctly.

Everyone has heard the term SEO at some point, but search engine optimization is a difficult and refined style of writing that requires a lot of up-front research. Each article you write, whether included on your own website to provide customers with added value or posted on other sites for linking purposes should be optimized with certain keywords designed to increase website traffic.

To determine which keywords will work best for you, take the time to research which words and phrases are most often searched for in relation to your products and services. If you can, choose a few and write different articles for each phrase.

Of course, developing your own Internet-based business can be very time consuming and you may need to call in the professionals now or somewhere down the line. Fortunately, there are many excellent companies that specialize in a range of techniques outlined above. If you don't have the time yourself, it's easy to find a group qualified and ready to research, set up links, and even provide professional writers to submit articles to market your site.

Whether or not you decide to use a professional, there's plenty you can do to optimize your site, get more business, and ultimately, if your business is floundering, turn your business around.

And now that we've looked at the internet and business turn around, it's time to enter the internet marketing environment and learn how to make the most of its natural features.

Chapter 4: Internet Marketing Environment

Imagine a visitor goes to your website, goes thorough the description of your products and services, and checks the pricing; makes up his mind to buy. The user is then required to check out your contact numbers and email to establish contact with you and place an order. Perhaps your phone was constantly busy and the enquiry mail landed up in your spam folder. You discover the e-mail after a week but by then your customer is either gone or hopelessly convinced that your level of customer service is terrible. Calculate the Lifetime Value of a customer and you can understand what's at stake.

What if your customer could buy directly from your company website?

Your website can be enabled to sell products online to customers anywhere in the world. Ecommerce makes it possible. Read on to know how to do it.

Elements of the Internet Marketing Evironment

Ecommerce
Ecommerce is all about sales and purchases over the Internet.

How does Ecommerce work?
Consumers who visit a website and decide to buy a product can buy with their credit cards. The money reaches you (the seller) and you in turn ship the goods or implement the services paid for.

Payment over the Internet is made possible by using a secure encryption method, which collects the personal and credit card details of the user. You can have them pay securely without having to worry about their credit card number known to others.

It is very much like shopping in a supermarket. You choose the goods you want to buy and keep collecting them in the "shopping cart". Once you are done, you proceed to check out and pay for the goods including the shipping cost. This information is then processed, which includes sending information to your credit card company or bank. The transaction is then approved or declined depending upon the verification of your details along with the funds available and your credit history. This authorization is a paid process and the information travels through a "Payment Gateway". The next step is to have the goods delivered to you. Hence for you as a seller, it would mean an added cost and an added feature for your customers.

Having a non-secure site would not only be a risky preposition for the customer, it will make you lose customers as well. They will not like to give away their personal and credit card details without being confident of the security.

How to enable your website for Ecommerce

If you are using template-based websites like the ones offered by www.moonfruit.com, you can opt for the Sitemaker Standard Package that offers Ecommerce tools as well. The annual subscription is below $100 per year (for complete website package which includes web hosting, designing tools as well).

If you are using an HTML-based website designed by a website designer, you need to contact your designer once again.

You should have:

SSL Certificate

An SSL or the "secure socket layer" certificate is used to protect the details of the conversation between you and your customer.

You may want to check out www.verisign.com and www.godaddyssl.com for the same. Price range starts from $100 per year.

You may also want to check out www.paypal.com as a free alternative to using an SSL or a shopping cart.

Shopping Cart

Shopping cart is a program, which keeps track of all the products that a customer chooses and compiles a list of the same along with the price when the user proceeds for check out. Simply put it is an electronic equivalent of the ones you use in shopping malls. Paypal again has free alternatives to the paid carts that can cost $500 upwards.

Consumers and the Internet Environment

When consumers visit a retail website, they want to feel that the information describing the products or services is accurate and unbiased. When they order and pay for a product online, they want to know that their financial records will be protected, that the product will be delivered on time, and that they can return something that is damaged or fails to meet their expectations. Most of the time, consumers don't know what level of security they are operating with.

Consumers make the vast majority of their online purchasing decisions almost solely on the basis of trust. Yet most websites provide consumers with very little reason to trust them! Worse than that, many websites look extremely untrustworthy; for example, some web retailers are start-ups with little or no track record of fulfillment. Some may have shaky financial footing and struggle to meet service and delivery guarantees.

Some online companies secretly collect data about each customer and their web activities. They go on to sell this information to third-party marketing firms. Even respected and established companies like AOL have suffered embarrassing security breaches; auction sites such as eBay have been scrutinized for their failure to police self-serving customer review posted by sellers and their friends.

Trust-based websites provide customers with accurate, up-to-date, complete, and unbiased information, not only on their own products, but on all the competitive products available in the market. Their smooth, easy-to-use navigation makes searching, shopping, and comparing a pleasure.

On top of this, they preserve and build trust with fulfillment and satisfaction guarantees. Trust-based websites enjoy higher rates of customer conversion and retention than sites that do not establish loyalty. Trusted websites promote customer loyalty and thereby enhance the lifetime value of their customers. If a company can master trust-based strategies it will go on to build a positive relationship with their customers as it also increases its market share and profits.

Leading sites are beginning to demonstrate some trust-building components. Virtual-advisor software, for example, mimics the behavior of a personal shopping assistant and can become a powerful and cost-effective part of almost any company's strategy to make the most of the online environment. However, before we consider the trust-building potential of virtual advisors, we will review established methods for generating trust online.

Trust is built in a three-stage, cumulative process that establishes trust in the Internet and the specific website, trust in the information displayed, and trust in delivery fulfillment and service. Trust in the information cannot be established until the website itself is trusted, and trust in fulfillment requires prior trust in the Web site and in the information it provides. Web trust cannot be established unless all three elements are well executed.

The keys to building website trust are:

- Maximize cues that build trust on your Web site.
- Use virtual-advisor technology to gain customer confidence and belief.
- Provide unbiased and complete information.
- Include competitive products.
- Keep your promises

Of course, trust is not the only element that makes a website a success. It can make all the difference, yes, but one of the most essential factors for a successful website is the ability to tap into a specific market niche. In chapter five, now that we know a little about the internet environment and the internet consumer, we will look at how to identify and tap a market niche to create the best possible strategies for yours business.

Chapter 5: Identifying Your Market Niches and Implementing Strategies

In any industry, your company has a major competitive advantage if you can identify what is known as a market niche for your business.

There is a need to shift from traditional modes of marketing (with "Brick and Mortar" infrastructures such as showrooms) to new ones which are more relevant and cost effective to SMEs (Small Medium Enterprises) in meeting existing market competition as well as to carve out new market niches. This presentation also highlighted some of the marketing resources available for SMEs to tap upon the implementation of its marketing and sales plans.

In an interview with Dr. Tian Yuan, Chairman of the China Chengtong Holding Company, Business-in-Asia quizzed him about the prospects for companies doing business in China via the internet? He replied as follows: We think the real successful companies in the Internet business in China will be those that can serve or combine their internet operations with other parts of their traditional businesses or industries ("old economy"). Businesses that solely have an internet focus without a production or other old economy element will find it very hard to succeed.

In a turnaround, where the improvement of the company is the goal, as well as in healthy companies trying to improve, the marketing and advertising potential of the internet is an attractive option. But the ones on the front lines of the world's businesses would agree with Dr. Tian Yuan, that the internet has NOT changed the way business is done.

Technology will never change the fact that a company has to know and trust who they are doing business with, confirm the quality of the products or services, and negotiate the best transaction. However, it is true that the internet has changed one thing clearly, and that is the relationship between the company and the customer. There is now the possibility of a direct line between the two and just not through dealers, agents, retail outlets, and distributors. A good example is Dell computers. What value will the internet give to my company? What value will it bring to my clients? What benefit is it to my company? These questions need to be clearly answered before taking the internet cure for the company's operations.

In planning the use of the internet as a global tool a company must realize that there are certain laws and limitations when one crosses a border—and this is true where one walks across a country border or crosses it electronically.

Just like in days of telefax, there are always the big ears to guard against—and security is a needed investment whether the system is an internal network system throughout the world or stands alone. In certain countries today certain words, products, services will draw governmental attention and in some cases get blocked. None of this is good for business. All of these cost money to prevent. The last thing a company needs when it is looking to expand its sales is to start out in a country with internet violations. There are border crossing these of both kinds: software that limits the internet and software that tries to skip the blocks. International efforts to govern this aspect of communication have so far not succeeded.

For a company to expect a turnaround from using the internet to sell its products it must first develop messages that are not subject to "Spam" filters and "Click Fraud Detectors". Most businesses and millions of potential customers now restrict messages severely to predetermined lists through Spam filters. In addition, if a message exceeds two clicks--three clicks (strikes) and you are out.

The future could well be that internet messages will only be received by the party welcoming them ahead of time.

A report from the Hitachi/Wharton School of Management indicates that internet is crucial to healthy as well as sick businesses. The day will soon be here when sales to customers and suppliers will require the internet for orders and sales completions. Internet usages have increased the productivity of companies by a considerable extent. And this is what a turnaround company exactly needs. Being in E-commerce is one of the first steps to rehabilitate some companies. Both Government and Industry are relying more and more on internet based orders. The whole use of design and product improvement with offshore companies is dependent upon the internet for communications. And this is one of the options we have presented for turnaround innovation.

Similarly problems of high cost of production and labour can also be improved via outsourcing and management using the internet. While internet, like all technologies has certain limitations and threats, no turnaround would be complete without a significant technological audit on how the company could improve by full utilization of the internet.

The internet can be a company's friend or foe. In the recent example of Proctor & Gamble in China it has been a big problem. Proctor & Gamble manufacture a product called SK II and the market in China for the product was strong and growing stronger as the Chinese family is able to purchase what was a formerly considered high luxury product just a few years ago. Proctor & Gamble estimates that 7% of their world sales came from China for the SK II product.

The product problem? Pressure from the government and the Chinese consumers that came after tests had shown that some samples of the product had caused some skin problems. How did the world get around? By internet, to thousands of potential Proctor & Gamble consumers. Blogs carried the message that caused the company to withdraw the product from the market as trust in the product was quickly lost. Management did not apologize and the destruction landed. The company, that had produced products that had been trusted by the Chinese consumers for many years, now faces a major need for turnaround.

The most important thing to remember and focus on when considering using the internet to conduct a sizeable percentage of your business: be thorough and conscious of the wider context in which you're operating. Develop a watertight strategy. Make the most of the advantages of online business; avoid the pitfalls.

Chapter 5: Internet Marketing Strategy

First of all, your internet marketing strategy should be included somewhere in your business plan to turn your company around. What does a business plan outline look like? Take a look:

This is an outline of a complete business plan:

Summary
Business Concept
Current situation
Key success factors
Financial situation/needs

Vision
Vision statement
Milestones

Market Analysis
The overall market
Changes in the market
Market segments
Target market and customers
Customer characteristics
Customer needs
Customer buying decisions

Competitive Analysis
Industry overview
Nature of competition
Changes in the industry
Primary competitors
Competitive products/services
Opportunities
Threats and risks

Strategy
Key competitive capabilities
Key competitive weaknesses
Strategy
Implementing strategy

Products/Services
Product/service description
Positioning of products/services

Competitive evaluation of products/services
Future products/services

Marketing and sales
Marketing strategy
Sales tactics
Advertising
Promotions/incentives
Publicity
Trade shows

Operations
Key personnel
Organizational structure
Human resources plan
Product/service delivery
Customer service/support
Facilities

Creating the financials of the business plan
Assumptions and Comments
Starting Balance Sheet
Profit and Loss Projection
Cash Flow Projection
Balance Sheet Projection
Ratio's and Analysis

Visit http://www.businesstown.com/planning/creating-rainbow.asp to see a complete sample of a business plan for a fictitious company. This should help you get your bearings and understand what you need to include for your plan to get the attention you want.

As for your internet marketing strategy, you should look to produce two additional plans that focus on particular areas of your primary business plan. The first plan is your marketing and sales. If you refer back to the content outline for the business plan, you can see that the marketing plan is going to focus attention on areas like marketing strategy, sales tactics, advertising, promotions and incentives, publicity, and trade shows. Your plans for using the internet should feature here. Your second plan - operations plan, should focus on areas such as key personnel, organization structure, and human resource plans, but you might also, as you go into more detail, include ideas for using the internet to generate further resources and manage customer service and support.

The Internet and Your Marketing Strategy: It isn't enough to build a website
You now know the importance of a website and how you can have one for your company.

However, having a great website with great design, speed, and content isn't enough. Now you need to make yourself heard on the web. You need to publicize your website, promote it – both on and off the net – drive traffic to it and ensure that the purpose for which you have created the website is fulfilled. The website must act the way you designed it

There are currently about 100 million websites and the number is constantly growing. If you are dumping your site on the net, it's unlikely many people will visit it. You need an established strategy to make people visit your website. You need to carefully apply resources.

Having a great website does not guarantee that somebody will visit it. You got to promote it: on visiting cards, emails, T-Shirts, in print everywhere.

(Detailed online advertising plan)

```
Company's Spending to serve a customer

By Phone = $33
Thru' Email = $9.99
Using Automated Web-based support = $1.72

Source: Forrester Research
```

Link Exchange Strategy
One of the no cost ways to promote your website is to exchange links with other websites. You may choose to email the webmaster of a particular site where you want to put up your link. A better way would be to first add the link of that website to yours and then make contact. This way it's a win-win situation and chances are good that your request to have your website link included someone else's site.

Linking is important because search engines go by the recommendations of popular websites. If a website with decent traffic has your link on to it, search engine will pick up that information and it increases your chances of showing up in search engine results. Another thing: the more links your site has, the greater are the chances that your site will rank highly on the search engine results.

It is important that you link only to those sites that compliment your business. Your traffic should be relevant to your business. If you run a car wash, putting up your link on to a calligraphy website is unlikely to bring you business.

Lead Generation: Viral Marketing

One of the best methods to the generate leads online is viral marketing.

Viral marketing refers to stealth marketing techniques that produce increase in brand awareness through a self replicating process. It is a technique for marketing that can increase exposure exponentially. It behaves in a very similar way to a computer virus in terms of the way that it spreads.

Through the Internet, it reaches a large number of people very quickly, executing a low cost marketing campaign to obtain response from a large number of interested people.

As a strategy, viral marketing encourages people to pass on marketing messages to their contacts and friends.

Viral marketing is the online equivalent of word-of-mouth marketing strategy.

Use viral marketing by establishing an offer – in short, concise, catching language – and establish your offer via e-mail (to customers and contacts) or via your website.

The invention of viral marketing is attributed to Hotmail.com. This was one of the first free email services and at the bottom of each of the free emails sent out was a small message 'Get your private, free email at hotmail.com.'

Implement a similar strategy and viral marketing can exponentially improve your leads.

Increasing Traffic
There are several ways to increase traffic to your website:

- Submit your URL to search engines
- Submit your URL to directories
- Announce your URL in Usenet newsgroups that may have an interest in the topic
- Add your URL to your business cards
- Add your URL to your stationery
- Publish flyers
- Publish it in newspapers, magazines, and other periodicals
- Publish it on all of your products
- Publish it on give-aways and trinkets
- Advertise on television and radio

You should add meta tags to your website and register with five of the more popular search engines, like www.google.com and www.yahoo.com. Less popular search engines will pick up on your company later.

Consider that approximately 55% of your Web traffic will come from search engine referrals. Optimize your webpages for search engine positioning and give your visitors a reason to return to your site.

Some more tips:
- √ Keep your pages fresh and current
- √ Reference your site and site references when writing an article you post
- √ Offer contests with prizes
- √ Offer a free e-book

All of these strategies are proven to increase web traffic to a site.

Exchanging Banners

Another method of generating more traffic is to exchange banners with one or more sites relevant to your business. As the name suggests, you place a banner ad for a particular site on your webpage. In turn, you can install a banner ad for your company on the site belonging to the advertiser on your site.

Ethical and Legal Issues

While the internet and internet marketing have raised a number of questions about ethical and legal issues related to online advertising and such, it is impossible to make clear determinations about the legal and ethical boundaries of online advertising. As yet, such boundaries are only loosely established.

United States government agencies like the Federal Trade Commission (FTC) have been assessing the legality and ethics of Internet advertising for several years. In March, 1996, it took action against nine companies for making false and unsubstantiated advertising claims in their Internet marketing. The Director of the FTC's Bureau of Consumer Protection called the Internet a new frontier for advertising and marketing but suggested the risks to its survival were substantial:

"The Internet will not achieve its commercial potential if this new frontier becomes the Wild West of fraudulent schemes. These FTC cases target deception in on-line marketing, and our focus on this area makes clear that the laws prohibiting fraud also apply to the information superhighway."
Jodie Bernstein, Federal Trade Commission

The Internet is a new frontier for marketing. The rules and regulations are rapidly evolving and in this environment, Internet advertisers need to be aware of the laws of their home country, as well as those which relate to other large market countries and international trade.

Advertisers are invited to be cautious and ensure that proposed advertising material is acceptable in key countries. They also strongly advise the prominent display of disclaimers on Web sites, and where appropriate the site should clearly state the countries to which an offer can only apply.

As the market for Internet advertising grows, it is inevitable that there will also be an increase in the number of advertisers who are neither honest nor responsible, attracted by a medium with the potential to reach a global market quickly and cheaply.

"The real problems are yet to emerge, as the bulk of consumers and merchants are currently kept out of the on-line marketplace by security concerns and payment difficulties. Once a secure, efficient and international model of digital payment is established it will be too late to step in and consider how best to impose regulation. Now is the time to recognise the promise and potential of electronic commerce and ensure it works for all Australian businesses, rather than leaving us behind, bound by the shackles of a paper based commercial system."
Melissa De Zwart, "Electronic Commerce: Promises, Potential and Proposals", University of NSW Law Journal.

As far as ethics goes in Internet advertising, experts tend to draw concerns about the following:

- *Online consumer research*
  Some efforts at online consumer research breach privacy rights of online consumers. Research efforts – surveys and the like – should respect user privacy and make an effort not to disclose personal information.
- *Marketing of professionals*
  Professionals marketing themselves online should only do so within the established ethical boundaries for their field.
- *Marketing to children and other vulnerable groups*
  Online advertisers should be aware that hard sell advertising to children and other vulnerable groups is unethical and in some cases illegal.
- *Marketing restricted products*
  Companies using online marketing tactics designed to appeal to teens for the purpose of promoting products like alcohol and tobacco should beware the ethical and legal implications of marketing restricted products.
- *Unsolicited commercials email or spam*
  The distribution of advertisements in the form of bulk emails should be undertaken with caution. Some online advertisement distribution companies are operating outside of the law in this regard.

It may be time to rethink the ethics of marketing on internet.
- Look to make advertising decisions that promote the greatest good for the mass consumers.
- Prima Facie duties framework
- Assume that there are inherent moral obligations relating to your decisions for an advertising campaign online
- Reflect on the intention, the means and the ends of your online marketing decisions

MARKETING STRATEGIES REVIEWED

Now that we've looked at some of the issues effecting specific internet marketing strategies, it's time to look at individual strategies, how they work, how you can achieve maximum benefit for your business, and how you can integrate specific strategies within a broader strategic context.

1) Email Marketing

"The Journey of a thousand miles begins with a single step"

Do you have an Email Address?

To start with your Internet Marketing plan, you don't need to splurge dollars making a website. Yes! Having a website isn't a fundamental requirement to get started. You can always have a website later. For now, a dedicated business email address can be used as your first step towards Internet Marketing. You don't need to spend any money. Moreover it will help you develop an understanding of the Internet Environment, which will come in handy when you make your website and own a place for yourself on the web!

Most of us have been using the Internet for years – for sending emails to family, friends, and work contacts; chatting, reading newspapers online, and so on. However, if your Internet use is limited to just that – it's like using a double barrel gun as a tool to scratch your back. You're still unaware of what Internet can do for you.

If you do not have an email address, you need to open an email account. There are plenty of companies that let you do this for FREE!

Getting an Email Address

Gmail from google offers you a lot of storage and is loaded with features that make emailing fast and fun. You may opt for another equally well-known service providers like Yahoo, Hotmail. You don't need expensive computer to get started.

A visit to your local store will help you find a system with basic components required to access the Internet. It won't cost you a fortune. Opt in for a broadband connection from your internet provider. There are several plans available, including unlimited monthly packages if you think you need it. Options like daytime only or nighttime only surfing are available. Choose the plan that suits your schedule for usage.

Best of the Web Free Email Accounts

The Table below will help you compare the services:

Why Email?

Here are the advantages of using Email as a medium of business communication.

- Cost Effective – You can cut costs dramatically by preferring Email over other medium of communication
- High ROI
- It's instant and it saves you a lot of time and money
- Proactive – You can actively distribute your e-mail whereas websites depend upon people visiting them
- Ideal for mass communication
- Conversational
- It is easier to reference
- Independent of geographical locations – kills distance
- Private
- Easy to Manage
- Easy to filter
- Secure and Reliable Transmission
- You can attach drawings, sounds, video clips, and other computer files to your e-mail.
- You can easily save thousands of e-mail messages, and you can search message files electronically.
- You can paste all or part of an e-mail into other computer documents.

Flipside

- Unsolicited Emails
- It can be a threat to the privacy of an organization as sensitive data might be accidentally or deliberately sent out to any number of people, anywhere – instantly.

You have an email now – What next?

No matter what business you are in, you would certainly like your potential customers out there to know that you exist. Traditional methods may involve taking out an ad in the print publications that have a circulation among your target audience. Traditional ads have some disadvantages, however:

- Print ads are costly
- Is not precise in reaching exclusively to your target audience
- It takes time to reach the audience
- It has very little lifespan

What if you start using email to communication with your potential customer? You will save see thousands of dollars on expensive ads in newspapers, printing flyers, greeting cards, and other offline promotional methods.

How to go ahead with your email

So now you are equipped to reach out to your prospects via email. You already have a great product; now you are ready to use the power of email to reach out to people and let them know about your product.

The way you communicate with your prospects is very important. It may well decide whether your prospect buys your product or not. Your email must have great content. Great content is not a matter of luck. There is a proven method. Let's check it out.

Top effective tips towards creating Great Email Content
- Include a short and snappy subject heading
- Use between 4 and 6 words in your subject heading
- Address your reader directly ("you", "your")
- Ensure the content is relevant and up-to-date
- Grab the attention of your audience
- Hold your audience with compelling argument or information they can use
- Remember that email is a marketing tool – treat it as one!

Now you have the power of content – Go out and Connect!

8 Billion is the number of emails which fly over the Internet worldwide in a year

The basic tool for Internet marketing – 'E-mail'

One of the most important tools that you will use in your Internet marketing is the electronic mail, better known as e-mail. It helps you to communicate with your visitors or customers easily, it is extremely inexpensive and it is much faster than snail mail.

You can go for any of e-mail programs programmes available on the Internet. For example, Eudora, which is a stand-alone e-mail program that can work with any Internet Service Provider (ISP). It provides you with a lot of features that can save you a huge amount of time. It will help you to easily organize your e-mail by filtering your messages into specific mailboxes. You can have your own domain for your e-mail address; it won't be someone else's.

Writing e-mail messages sounds pretty simple, but there are important aspects that need to be taken care of.

1) **Subject line**: Grabbing your readers' attention is a very important factor. Just because the visitor is your customer or a buyer, it doesn't mean that he/she will open your message. They should be intrigued to open up your mail. You must be able to steal their attention. And to achieve this attention, the subject of your e-mail, which is the most important part of your message, should be short, to the

point, and should provide a summary or a zest as to what your message is all about.

2) **Format of your message**: Many people have a confusion that which format should they follow for their e-mail, HTML or text. Although there has been a lot of controversy on this, text message is the better option. The reason for this is that not all your readers will be capable of viewing your e-mail messages in HTML format. But even then, if you want to go for HTML messages, the best way to accommodate all your readers is to create two versions and allow them to make the choice themselves.

3) **Line length**: Some e-mail programs do not have the feature of automatic text wrap. So, even if your message looks pretty good to you, it is very possible that your e-mail recipient may receive your message as one long sentence, which looks unpleasant. So, as you start writing your e-mail message, you should keep this in mind that your line length should be limited under 65 characters per line. Use the hard carriage return at the end of each line. If you don't feel like formatting your text by yourself, you can accomplish this online:-
http://www.web-source.net/format_text.htm.

4) **Linking:** When you place a web address in your messages, some e-mail programmes automatically create live links with web addresses starting with 'www.'. However, some e-mail programmes are able to create live links only when the web address begins with 'http://'. Hence, you should always include the full URL beginning with http://.
When you are including an e-mail address within your e-mail message, you should always include 'mailto:' directly in front the e-mail addresses. This will enable most e-mail programs to create a live e-mail link.

Try to keep you web addresses short, so that the URL doesn't get divided into into two different lines, which may cause only a part of the web address to become a live link.

E-mail marketing

E-mail marketing is mailing to targeted mass via electronic mails. In an e-mail newsletter, all the content comes from you. For attorneys, consultants, social workers, decorators, and other professionals, this is a perfect way to cultivate loyal fans of your expertise. When you write it in a tone and fill it with customer centered content, you maintain top of mind awareness among subscribers and win new recruits for your fan club through the pass along factor.

There are many purposes of e-mail marketing, like advertising to recruit new clients, introducing new set of products or services to an existing client base.

E-mail advertising is far more cost effective than direct marketing through regular mail, telemarketing or door to door sales.

Retain your old clients

Repeat customers contribute 60% of the annual income to most of the online companies. If you constantly try to attract new customers and get market share away from your competitors, you may forget your existing customers and they will forget you. And you may lose your source of profitable sales. You can run an e-letter campaign. You can send business cards or e-letters to all your existing customers. You can market to your existing clients easily by following a number of strategies:

1) Repeat: Success in business, whether it's an online or offline business, depends on your commitment to delivering newsletters and other marketing material consistently. Sending e-mails or your company's newsletters on a regular basis is a very reproductive method to send out your message to your customers. Depending on how often your customers decide to buy products or services, you can decide the frequency of sending out your e-mails or letters.

2) Steal attention: If you want each of your marketing tactic to positively support your online company, the key feature is quality. Hence the messages you create should be meaningful, relevant, and interesting to the reader. Your message should include some interesting graphic elements. Your e-mail campaign can offer expert advice, entertaining and eye catching features, and special discounts available only via your e-letter. You can always outsource this if you don't have anyone on your staff capable of creating this material for you.

E-mail newsletter
If there are no potential prospects or a list of people who opted in to receive your messages, instead you use a list that you bought, or you are doing it without warning the people on your list, then you are sending a spam; you are considered a spammer. And once you are labeled a spammer, you will be put on millions of black lists. And it very hard to get out of it.

Don't take this risk; use opt-in e-mails only.

And, lastly, you can outsource to a company that professionally does the job of automation. It will be very tedious for you to send thousands of e-mails, managing lists, subscribing and unsubscribing people. Automation is the best solution.

A wonder of e-mail marketing – "Opt-in mailing list"
A mailing list is nothing more than a plain text file containing email addresses.

You may be dubious about asking your potential customers for their e-mail addresses. Opt-in e-mail list consists of e-mail addresses of the customers given to you willingly. The customer asks you to send them newsletters, ezines, e-courses, special offers, and discounts. Anything else is called spam.

With the help of opt-ins, you can maximize your sales by presenting your offers to willing customers. You can establish an electronic, permission based, relationship with loyal visitors and customers.

If you are depending hits only, you're in trouble. Visitors don't usually buy the first time they visit a website. Studies say that a typical Internet customer will visit a site seven times before deciding to buy a product from that website.

You can convert one-time visitors into your best customer. Opt-in e-mails will help you to improve and enhance your advertisements, creating more sales. You can build up a relationship with your customer, so they will come back for more.

Most e-mail addresses are submitted to lists via a form on a website. There are varieties of ways you can convince people to subscribe to your list:

1) **Offer free newsletters:** People love to receive information. They pay for information. If you can provide potential subscribers with information they need, and if you can do this for free, they will be glad to subscribe to your newsletter. Offering free newsletters is the best way to collect opt-in e-mail addresses. With the help of this service, you can build up a credible relationship with potential customers.

2) **Offer free e-books:** This will help you to grow your online business and get more subscribers. But the e-book you provide should have quality information. Otherwise you may lose customers. If you don't let their interests go away, and you draw them to your services, you will have returned visits from these loyal customers. Most important, you will have their e-mail addresses.

3) **Offer free article about your products and services:** If you have a quality product for sale, or if your services are one of a kind, you can send people free articles giving details of your products or services. This is a very powerful tactic and an excellent way to building up your opt-in e-mail list.

4) **Provide the customer with free download:** If you are selling software, you can give away the trial version of your software for free. When they are downloading the trial version, they should be offered to special discounts on the full version, which would need their e-mail addresses. And you have hit the jackpot.

An extremely important factor: People must be able to unsubscribe whenever they want no further e-mails from you. Otherwise you will be accused of spamming.

What To Look For In An E-Mail Marketing Company?

1) Automation of your subscribe and unsubscribe requests: As it has been told earlier that it is very beneficial to have a subscription form in your website, which allows you to get e-mail address and contact information of your customer. Now imagine you have to create this subscription form yourself. Seems like a very time consuming job. Instead, you can go for e-mail marketing companies that will provide you with exact HTML code you need to paste to your website to have a subscription form in your site. For better services, you can also attach a link at the bottom of your subscription form that helps the subscribers to update their information in the form or unsubscribe from a list. These e-mail marketing companies can automate everything for you.

2) Personalize your e-mails: You can merge capabilities to personalize every e-mail that you send. This is another powerful feature of many e-mail marketing services. In addition to the standard first name and last name, custom fields are also included by better services.

3) Bounce back e-mail handling: Imagine that all your non-deliverable e-mails be sent back to you, it will be a big nuisance if your list is large. These e-mails that are sent to e-mail accounts that no longer exist or are full or blocked, are called bounce backs. And if you continuously send out e-mails with bounce backs, you may enter the list of spammers. This should be avoided at all costs. You can use softwares that have the capability to remove these bounce back mails. Whenever a bounce back is received, the software makes a note of the address and if another bounce back is received the e-mail address will be sent to a list of dead addresses.

4) HTML e-mail: Most e-mail marketing companies support the ability to send out HTML e-mails; messages that include graphics and formatted text. You can go for HTML e-mails. Perhaps, not all users have the ability to view e-mail messages in HTML format. So it's very easy for you to get listed into the spammers since your HTML e-mail may make no sense to them. To avoid this, look for companies that use multi-part MIME to send out messages. When you send an HTML email in multi-part MIME, users who do not have the ability to view HTML messages will receive the e-mail in the usual text format.

Free Email Newsletters
Since email is a no cost proposition, it's a good idea to develop a database of prospects so you can contact them, informing them about new products and services from time to time. This greatly increases the chances of making a sale.

Now how do you make people give you their email address? It's simple. Just tell them to enter their name address and email to download a free newsletter. Your newsletter should be attention-worthy and must contain something of use to your target.

With ezines and newsletter for your target audience you can get into instant communication with hundreds of prospects and customers at practically no cost. You will see your email database growing. Just think how much effort and money it would have cost you to build a database the traditional way. This size of your customer database might as well predict the success or failure of your business. You may now keep sending information on regular updates, events, new products, promotions festive offers and what not.

Out of sight is out of mind. Your newsletters help your prospects keep you in mind while they make a purchase.

Be consistent: Your mailing list is one of the most powerful marketing tools. It pays to be consistent with your newsletters. You can choose to send one general information-based newsletter once a month initially followed by another one describing your products, their features, prices, and discount offers.

Initially as the list is growing, you might be able to continue mailing your prospects, but, as the list grows, it starts getting difficult to manage the database and mailings. Outsourcing email management will help you offload and have the energy to focus on your core issues. Application service providers (ASPs) can manage your database and related activities. Using a professional service would enable you to send 5000 to 10000 newsletters or ezines per month.

Opt-In email

When a prospect visits your site and willingly gives his email address to download your free newsletter, you have an opportunity to ascertain his willingness to receive further informative emails from you. There can be an option to click on a box if the user wants to hear from you later. This way the user has given you consent to establish communication and registered interest in receiving informative emails such as newsletters, offers, and product info via email.

This type of mail, for which the user gives his consent or permission, is called Opt-In or a permission-based-email-list.

Sending emails to an email address without permission is taken as spam. Spam has no use for the user and is more of a bother. If you have a legitimate permission from the user to send him bulk email, it is perfectly legal. However if you are sending emails to a certain email address without the user's consent it is illegal and is considered spamming.

Spam Free E-Mail Campaigns – Ad Testing

The best way to use e-mail to develop your online business is by creating a double opt-in list on Yahoo Groups, or Topica.com, or Free Lists.org.

Double opt-in list

A double opt-in list means that a subscriber requests the mailing then receives a verification email from the mailing list telling him that he must follow certain steps to verify his intentions to subscribe. Double opt-in is a method of getting someone to agree twice to receive e-mails in the future.

Avoid single opt-in lists, since they are often abused.

There are a several companies out there with double opt-in mailing lists for ads, but be very cautious while selecting any of these companies. There are a lot of crooks that send spam to millions of customers. If the company cannot validate their double opt-in mailing lists and if they are not able to get their clear references, leave them.

Ezine advertising
Each of the hosting companies allows you to place an ad in each mailing delivered to your group.

The key to any opt-in list is to provide anything of top notch. That can be the only probable reason why people will sign up to receive your information. You can provide valuable information with the help of ezines also. And by constantly providing your readers with valuable information, you can build up a relationship with people who would actually like to buy some of your products.

Ezine advertising is a great way to build up your business. But learning where to place your ads takes time. Most of the ezines don't have a buyer list; rather they are all comprised sellers who were searching for free sample advertisements. Similarly, you can use them to test your ads before giving money to the paid ezines.

Other ways
There are other ways to test your ads, for example, place them in classified ad websites, safe-lists,general advertising or niche mailing lists. You can run them in low-cost ezines. With the help of ezines, you can provide some type of valuable information of interest to your target market.

Sites like http://SubmitAds.net permit you to place your ads in their directory and then send your message to people who will place their advertisements through your replicated SubmitAds website.

You can also set up your ads as independent doorway pages that are submitted to the search engines.

No matter what approach you take to place your ad, you should always take some testing steps. Otherwise your results would be based upon guesswork only.

Try to search which ad tracking software is best suited for your business, and use them for testing. By testing your ads and advertisement mediums, analyze the results produced by each. Discard the option that was not successful to produce satisfactory results and move on with the best.

A few terms you should know
Opt-Out email
Unconfirmed Opt-In
Confirmed Opt-In
Opt-Out Bulk Email

Use the power of referrals
You may consider including a "Forward to friend" option in the newsletters or ezines you send. It can be a very good way to expand your emailing database at no cost.

Tips For Creating An Impeccable E-Mail Message

With electronic business messages, you have to consider some essential dos and don'ts, similar when you talk to someone face to face or on the telephone.

Your good manners can always help you to build up good business relationships. And therefore you should keep in mind: -

Use your real names in your messages:
Your customers, who are the recipients of your messages, should have an impression that they are communicating with a human being, not any company ID. Your e-mail address may not indicate your name, but your message can. Not giving your name sounds rude to the recipient.

Don't annoy people:
You should not excessively use the technology of e-mail, just because it is for free. It becomes a burden for your customer to receive and go through tons of e-mails in a short period of time.

Don't overburden your recipient:
An e-mail that goes on for pages and pages gets very tiring to be read on the computer screen by the recipient. Hence your messages should have a limited length with all the details included.

Don't give a burden with your jokes and alerts:
You should always remember that you are doing a business proposition and including fun in your messages should stay within limits. Too many jokes may give an impression to the recipient that you are not that professional.

Don't say x, but offer y:
You should never use the words like "Hi" or "Hello" when you are mailing a newsletter about your latest products. Moreover, if you tell him what he should probably do with your product rather than offering him the advantages of the item, you sound over hyped to the customer.

Be professional in you messages:
Your messages should be professional; use complete sentences, check the spellings and the grammar; use capitals in the standard way, be as clear and simple as possible, and don't use slang language.

Don't send attached files:

There are many people who don't have any idea what to do with non-text files .And even if your customer knows how to open an attached file and read it, they will have to go to a lot of trouble. If you are sending an attached file, you should do so with prior agreement, and the file should be worth opening. Prior agreement is required because if the customer doesn't know you, he may think that there is virus in your attachment.

Hide multiple addresses:
If you are sending one particular mail to multiple people, you would probably use carbon copies..,Don't have a huge list of e-mail addresses before the actual body of the message. This is quite annoying for each of the recipient. As a solution, you can use blind carbon copies, where the list of e-mail addresses is not seen anywhere.

Automation of your ordering and fulfillment process
When you have just started with your business, you will find it very pleasing to handle all the incoming orders yourself. It is because you will find out that your hard work is paying off and it satisfies you to see those first few sales and you tend to look in to all the questions, e-mails and orders of your customer yourself, personally.

But, as your business expands and you start receiving hundreds and thousands of orders, the initial exciting period is over and you won't find handling them yourself a fun.

This is where automation comes in. Your sales and ordering process is very crucial part of your business and it is important to automate it from the beginning, without which your business won't grow.

Automation of your ordering and fulfillment process can easily boost your sales by 30%, overnight. Online customers are very demanding towards the quality of the services they are being provided with. They would want to buy your products online and receive those items as quickly as possible.

It is extremely advantageous for you to build happy satisfied customers. If you can make it easy for your customers to order and receive your products, you have an edge against your competitors. This can be achieved by automating your ordering and receiving process.

Moreover, you are making the whole process hands free so that you can concentrate on the growth of your business.

You can now spend time on writing order confirmations, send thank you messages to your customers and up an impression.

Auto responders can manage all your time consuming tasks:
- Buyers always want to be reassured that their order has gone through successfully. You can setup an auto responder that sends an e-mail message to the customer confirming that their orders are safe and processing. Receiving an instant confirmation from you stops the customer from calling and e-mailing

again and again for reassurance. It will give the impression that you are running a highly professional business.

- Buyers also tend to make phone calls and e-mails asking if the product has been shipped. An auto responder that confirms shipment of a product can help you save yourself from this trouble. Notifying the customers that their order has been shipped can also create a good impression.

- You can also create an auto responder to e-mail your customer a link from where they can download software or an information product like an e-book. Even this technique is very satisfying for the customer.

- It will of course take a lot of your crucial time to send e-mail to each of your customer after the sale of each product thanking them to buy the product from you. An auto responder can accomplish even this job. In addition you can also send them information about related products. With no work on your part you can sell your back end products also.

Benefits of having an Online Newsletter
- Inexpensive: Like most things online, e-newsletters won't set you back a whole lot. Producing and distributing newsletters is cost-effective. The costs of printing and mailing are completely eliminated.

- Cuts Design Time: Once you've designed the layout for your first e-newsletter – once you are happy with it – you can keep your template for your future issues. It's easy to update e-newsletter templates and, saving time is also saving money.

- Expedient Distribution: You can mail out your e-newsletter very quickly. There's no time to be delivered; compare to the two or three days it takes to deliver most mail packages via the postal service. Being able to create and deliver your e-newsletter so quickly also means that the content is unlikely to have lost any relevance.

- Increased Chance of Being Read: Numerous studies show that e-newsletters are more likely to be read than traditional paper newsletters. The e-mail distribution method allows you to target your audience and a targeted audience means more readers.

Tips for creating an Online Newsletter
- Use graphics sparingly

- Use multi-column layouts

- Divide the text – don't let it run across the screen

- Focus on marketing your product or service by focusing on benefits

Free Ezines
An abundance of free online newsletters is available online. Internet users subscribe to these newsletters and receive them free as emails.

There are plenty of ways to draw attention to your site and your business using these e-mail newletters.

- Find e-zines that allow you to place free ads for your business
- Write articles for free ezines to publicize your business
- Submit your ezine to ezine directories
- Use ezine announcement lists to promote your own ezine and your business

Database Marketing
This is a method of collecting all available information about customers, leads, and prospects and compiling that information in a single database. Companies use databases to continually gather, refine, and analyze data about customers, reviewing such things as buying history, prospects, past marketing efforts, demographics, and the like. The data is analyzed and the information reviewed so the company can make informed decisions about marketing and sales in the future.

The companies that use database marketing include some of the most successful online marketers of the day. Dell Computer, for example, and Lands' End use database marketing to send targeted promotional offers, assess the value of individual customers, and track the all-important return on investment values for their marketing ventures.

2) Search Engine Optimization

How does a customer know you exist?

A typical offline business spends a great percentage of the marketing budget on newspaper and magazine adverts, flyers, billboards, and more to be "visible" to a potential customer. What is "seen" is what is "bought".

Similarly a typical surfer depends heavily on Search Engines like Google, Yahoo, MSN, Hotbot, AOL, Lycos, WebCrawler, or any other popular one to look out for information on a particular product or service. A search engine is like the genie on the Internet - always ready to obey your command. You tell the search engine what you want and the search engine promptly gets it.

All the surfer needs to do is to visit any search engine and type in his query and press Enter. Within seconds the search engine comes up with hundreds and thousands of results matching the query. The results are web pages from various sites on the Internet, which contain information matching the keywords in the query along with the websites URL. Clicking on a result leads you to the specific website for detailed information. The user can then check whether he has found the information he was looking for or not. If he is not satisfied with the result, he may consider checking other results. Or else he may alter the keywords and try again to get different results.

For example you are into the business of providing consultancy to small businesses. Does your site show up as a prime result of an Internet Search when a surfer tries to find a list of consultants? If no, you are seriously missing out on many opportunities for business because you are not visible. When you are not visible nobody knows about you and you don't get any business even if you are providing excellent services.

The question now is "How does my company's website appear high in the results?" To know more about it, we must first get to know how a search engine works.

How Do Search Engines Find Information

Search Engines are huge searchable databases of resources extracted from the Internet by the process of "crawling". This is just like sending the genie to crawl over all the resources and return with the resources that match the word and phrases (keywords) in the user's query. These resources are then sorted out and displayed in the results according to probable relevancy. The most relevant resources or websites are ranked high and hence are displayed in the top results (the very first page).

Factors which are known to affect the ranking of a particular resource (website) include:

- ✓ Web Content Factors

  - Word Frequency
  - Location of keywords in the document
  - Number of pages in the site containing the keywords (Relational Clustering)
  - The time taken by the website to load

- ✓ External Factors

  - Link popularity
  - Link relevancy
  - Click popularity
  - Length of stay
  - Length of domain
  - Demographic popularity
  - Frequency of Updates
  - Google Page rank
  - Results from partner search site are ranked higher
  - Paid placements are ranked high

Different search engines have different techniques and programming for creating database, therefore each search engine has its own database which is different from the other. Search Engines can hence be differentiated into "Crawler Based" like Google, "Human Powered Search Directories" like open directories, or mixed.

The challenge ahead is to have your website among one of the top results generated by the search engine – to be perfect bait for the crawling spider. Put enough spider food on your site. In other words, you need to optimize your content to make sure that your website is noticed by the search engine and placed high up in the results so that it gets visible to your prospective customers wanting information on the products and services you sell.

What if you have the right content which your potential customers are searching right there in your website? It increases the chances of your site being picked up by the search engine and eventually get visited by more and more potential customers. Isn't it what you want?

Search Engine Optimization or SEO is a proven method to push your ranking high up in the search results. Let us know more about it.

Search Engine Optimization
Though there are several advanced techniques for Internet Marketing, search engines are as much relevant as they were years ago. This is because Search Engines act like an entry point on the web for most users looking for information. The fact that your website shows up in the web search is still the most promising tool of attracting prospects to your business to know about the products and services you have to offer. Search Engine Optimization or SEO of your website, therefore, must not be taken lightly.

Search Engine Optimization (SEO) means anticipating the keywords which the user would use to search information across a search engine, and placing these keywords in strategic locations across your website to attract a search engine.

These strategic locations of your website are:

- The domain name
- The page title
- The alt tags
- The keywords meta-tags
- The description meta-tags
- The comments tag
- The robots Tag

Your website creators would be able to do this for you.

It is therefore critical:

- To choose the right keywords which promise maximum "hits" to your website
- To use the right title tag
- To have your website designed and set up correctly
- To have the right content – It's no point working so hard to get a visitor to your website, when he cannot find anything of use in it.

Taking care of the procedures above will ensure that your website is now optimized for Search Engines. The better the optimization, the better the chances of your website being ranked better by search engines and get visited by prospective customers.

The next step now is to submit or register your website to various search engines.

Search Engine Submission
You can submit your site to search engines for free or via the paid search engine programs. You need to go to search engines and look out for the "Suggest a site" or "Add URL" button. Then type in your website address there and you are registered.

Now whenever a surfer would use keywords matching your site, the title and description of your website would appear among the results and the chances of your site getting visited gets better and better.

You can submit your site to specialized directories as well. If you are an event management company you better get listed for a web directory of entertainment and event management companies.

Free Search Engine Submission Sites

Search Engine/Directory

1. Google
   http://www.google.com/addurl/?continue=/addurl
2. Yahoo! Search
   http://search.yahoo.com/info/submit.html
3. MSN
   http://search.msn.com/docs/submit.aspx?FORM=WSDD2
4. Open Directory Project
   http://dmoz.org/
5. www.submitexpress.com/submit.html
6. Exact Seek
   http://www.exactseek.com/add.html
7. AOL
8. Alta Vista
9. All the Web
10. Yahoo Direct
11. Looksmart

12. Search Site
    http://searchsight.com/submit.htm
13. www.quickregister.et
14. Buzzle
    http://www.buzzle.com/suggest_basic2.asp
15. www.submitawebsiteWebsite.cm/free_submission_top_engines.htm
16. ww.buildtraffic.com/submit_url.shtml
17. www.addpro.com/submit30.htm
18. www.nexcomp.om/weblaunch/urlsubmission.html
19. http://selfpromotion.com/?CF=google.aws.add.piyw
20. www.submitcorner.com/Tools/Submit/

Paid Submission

One of the major players in paid submission today is Google AdWords. Here you decide on the keywords most relevant to your business. You can then have your advert placed right on the page where the results would be displayed for a particular keyword search. You pay only and only if the visitor while scanning through the result page, notices your ad and clicks it to reach your website. In case the surfer does not click on your advert, you don't pay. To be precise, you pay per click.

Yahoo Search Marketing is another similar pay per click program where your advert is displayed along with search results on the keyword chosen by you. Like in Google Adwords, you pay only when you are "hit"

This type of PPC or CPC (Paid Per Click and Cost Per Click respectively) advertising is known as *"Search Advertising"*.

The effectiveness of this type of advertising can be ascertained from the fact that Yahoo and Google not only sell these ads on their search engines but as well as through their network of other search engines and other websites like ESPN, Lycos, AOL, The New York Times, MSN, Alta Vista, CNN, and many more. Though many people still prefer "Organic" results of a search engine than Pay per Click, the number of people clicking on adverts is increasing.

The critical requirement for the success of Search Advertising is the right choice of the keyword. Using tools like wordtracker.com would not only help you research the right keywords, but will also educate yourself on major and minor keywords, tell the "hot" keyword by letting known the number of times a particular keyword is searched, keyword combinations, and more.

Advantages of Search Advertising
-   The advertisers pay only when their advert is actually clicked by the surfer and is led to their site thereby ensuring that they get value for money.

- The surfers clicking on the adverts are the ones who are already searching information on the same keywords. The businesses thus have a clear advantage of getting attention to their target audience.
- By getting your ad displayed in Google Adwords and Yahoo Search, businesses can reach maximum number of Internet users in a very short time thereby making huge savings on time, effort and money. Google, Yahoo and MSN constitute about 90% of the search results.
- You can spread the word around about your business in no time.
- Businesses don't need to worry about spam. Surfers decide to visit your site or not.
- The copy of the ad can be changed, modified, or stopped anytime.
- You can even place more than one advert of yours.
- Websites built on high end software like flash (for eg, if you choose to make your site with www.moonfruit.com) can really benefit from their ads getting displayed along with search results as search engine crawlers have difficulty listing flash sites.

Contextual Advertising

This kind of advertising involves placing relevant ads on the advertising space of various web pages a surfer would browse looking for information. It is based on the logic you must be able to get noticed while a surfer is looking for specific product or services in the line of your business. Though the chances of a surfer actually buying your product may be less than in search advertising, it's a good way to add your brand to the knowledge of the surfer so that it helps them make a buying decision later.

Over 70% of internet users prefer to use the natural "organic" results of a search engine and by using an SEO Consultant you can gain significant traffic over a long-term period and achieve sales and enquiries at a much lower cost than PPC over a longer period.

Using Site Submission Software

http://www.sitesolutions.com/
http://www.mikes-marketing-tools.com/directory/search-engine-submission-software.html
http://www.submissionpro.com/
http://www.submiturl.com/
http://www.axandra-web-site-promotion-software-tool.com/search-engine-submission.htm
http://www.instantposition.com/offers/toprankings.html?gclid=CO2zypv8togCFR5fTAo
dLR5Q9Q

Getting Professional Help – Hiring a SEO company

SEO requires adequate knowledge, effort, time, certain expertise, and experience. In addition you must be equipped to monitor the progress and keep an eye on your rankings on almost a daily basis. If you have the budget to hire a professional SEO company, you may rather consider entrusting the job to them so that you don't make costly mistakes and your inexperience does not waste time.

There are many SEO companies on the net which take care of website submission to hundreds of search engines, optimizing content, positioning, and would also offer help on bid management, branding, PPC advertising and so on.

Outsourcing SEO function may give you more time to other core issues while the SEO Company actually executes your SEO plan.

Before you entrust the job to a particular company you may want to check its reputation, work expertise, customer care, work ethics and their own ranking at the search engine results!

Some Optimizations tips

1. Place spider food all along your site. Use keywords heavily. Place key phrases within the first 25 words of your site. Keywords must have around 5% - 7% density.
2. Website design must be to the liking of search engines. Prefer HTML and text over graphics and other page formats. A site made in Macromedia Flash would make it difficult for the search engine to crawl through them.
3. A site map may not be of great use to visitors but helps the search engine to properly index your pages in its database.
4. Use Copyright and About Us pages. Link all web pages to home page as well.
5. Every page must have a static link of its own. Websites made on flash are at a disadvantage here.

Measuring your SEO progress

Did you ever wonder if there is a way to know the status of the ranking of your website at various search engines databases? Or if you had something which could analyze your site and let you know if you are using keywords rightly? Or is your site's loading speed ok or do you need some corrective measures?

Here are some resources that will help you measure your SEO performance.

www.wwebsiteoptimization.com/services/analyze
Analyzes speed, size etc and advises accordingly

www.mikes-marketing-tools.com/ranking-reports
This is an excellent tool that gives you in a tabular format your sites rankings in top search engines for free.

www.nichebot.com
Keyword analysis tool

In addition to these www.wordtracker.com helps you find the right keyword. It offers trial offers; www.searchengineworld.com is again an excellent resource for SEO related tools and offer keyword density analysis testing.

More about directories
The Open Directory Project (ODP) like DMOZ.org, built by human volunteers is a worldwide website directory. You can submit your site to open directory as you do for a search engine submission. However, utmost care must be taken to submit the site in the right category or else your site will not show up.

3) The Joint Venturing on the Internet

Overview: Joint Venturing on the Internet
What is joint venturing and how does it help your business? Two very simple questions to which there are hardly simple answers. A joint venture, in the real world or offline, is considered to be any venture undertaken by two or more organizations as a partnership or comglomerate. The basic idea is that two or more organizations take action together, sharing risks and, if all goes well, sharing in the profit acquired from the venture.

Most joint ventures, off- and online are undertaken by companies that have, between them, a whole range of expertise.

Sometimes called a host-beneficiary relationship, or strategic alliance, a joint venture is a business process and a subtle form of marketing, based on a form of loose partnership with another company or with a number of companies.

This form of marketing utilizes existing customer relationships and goodwill that other companies have already established within a market base. The basic concept is that two or more businesses give each other access to their respective customer pools, which allows both of the joint venture partner to leverage each other's assets and resources for mutual benefit.

In most online joint ventures, of which banner advertising is a particularly popular variety, you can promote the products and services of your joint venture partner or partners to your customers. In exchange, your joint venture partner promotes your products and services to his customers. To show your gratitude, you give each other a portion of the profits from the resulting sales.

Joint venturing is a great way to tackle a specific group of people with whom another company is already dealing.

Perhaps the best thing about this business process and marketing model is that you have considerable freedom to choose who you deal with, and you can deal with your competitors just as easily as with non-competitors.

Benefits of Joint Venture

Joint venture is one of the most effective ways of enhancing your relationship with subscribers and customers. It'll reflect positively on you if you're able to find a quality product and service at an excellent value to offer them and you will do a lot for your business by earning the respect and cooperation of other established companies. You get a stamp of approval when you achieve a successful joint venture.

Above all, you should emphasize to your customer base the amazing value you are securing for them by entering into a joint partnership They must believe that you've gone out of your way to find the offer and pass it on to them, and when they believe this, you'll find they are more likely to buy into whatever you decide to offer to your customers that's from your competitors..

On the other hand, if the products and services you offer your customers are substandard and don't add much value to your business, your venture is likely to backfire. When you're long-time customers think you're out to make a fast buck out, they are unlikely to support you..

That said, when it's done right, joint venturing helps you increase the size of your opt-in and ultimately the size of your customer base very quickly. It's not uncommon to add hundreds of new subscribers to your list within minutes of launching your joint venture.

You can gain instant credibility by leveraging on the good name of your joint venture partner. If your partner is reputable, and commands the trust of his subscribers and customers, this goodwill will be passed on to you.

The fact that your joint venture partner is endorsing your products and services makes his subscribers and customers think you're credible as well. This is called gaining credibility and goodwill through association.

You're guaranteed of increased response because your sales message is certain to be read by your joint venture partner's subscribers and customers. This is third party endorsement at play here. Your joint venture partner has already established a relationship with his subscribers and customers and they're likely to trust his endorsement as opposed to you trying to sell your products/services to them yourself.

Joint venture is a great way to acquire new subscribers and customers with practically no costs. It allows you to leverage your joint venture partner's traffic, existing subscribers and customers. You don't have to incur expenses in acquiring new traffic and you can be pretty certain that the traffic you get from your joint venture partner is targeted and therefore likely to be profitable.

Another benefit is that it allows you to offer new products to your existing subscriber and customer base if you don't have any products to sell, or you don't want to incur the expense of developing new products.

You could do an endorsement of your joint venture partner's products to your existing subscriber and customer base. This can be extremely profitable because your subscribers and customers will think that it's a valuable product otherwise you wouldn't have endorsed it, especially if you've a good reputation with them. They're unlikely to think that you're trying to make a fast buck out of them.

Find out who sells to your target market, what products and services they're selling, and who your target market trusts and has good relationship with. You'll then want to contact them to establish a joint venture deal. Offer them complementary products and services. This is a win-win proposition because it adds another profit stream. If yours is a reputable company that offers high quality products and services, it should be really easy for you to find other companies to partner with.

Here are some examples of Joint Venture deals that you can go into:

1. Complementary Services or Products
If you sell accounting software to small businesses, you could contact those who sell computer hardware to small businesses to cut a joint venture deal. In this case, both you and your potential joint venture partner are serving the same small business market. Furthermore, both your products are complementary which makes it ideal to enter into a partnership.

You can promote computer hardware to your accounting software customers and prospects, and your joint venture partner can do the same by promoting your accounting software to their existing customers and prospects.

2. Percentage Profit Sharing
If you've a great product but don't have a big subscriber and customer list, and website traffic, you could approach those who've a great list or a high traffic website to cut joint venture deals with. Your joint venture partners can promote your great product to their list in exchange for a percentage of profits from the resulting sales.

3. The co-development of products
You might have specialist knowledge with high demand but you may lack product creation skills. You could easily approach someone who is good at creating products, such as, ebooks, tapes and videos, to strike a joint venture deal. You can provide the specialised knowledge whilst your joint venture partner can be responsible for creating the products.

4. Ezine-Based Promotions
You can also enter into a list building joint venture with ezine publishers where all partners promote each other's ezine at the subscription 'thank you' page. After someone has subscribed to your ezine, you'll redirect them to the subscription thank you page where you display your joint venture partners' ezines.

The major plus of joint venture marketing is that it benefits all parties involved. It is a definite win-win business proposition. You win, your joint venture partners win, and your customers and subscribers win. Joint venturing is very low cost and low risk, and is one of the fastest ways of bringing your product to market.

Do it right, joint ventures can literally explode your online sales and profits.

4) Banner Advertising Online

Banners are very similar to the roadside billboards advertisers display to make consumers aware of their client's products and services. It helps consumer aware of the products available in the market and may go ahead and buy the same.

Using banner advertising on the Internet is very much the same. You place banners on various websites with complimentary businesses. Surfers get routed to the advertiser's website by clicking the banner which has a hyperlink to your site.

The banner advertising can be successfully converted to a pay per click system as well. You pay only when a surfer clicks the banner and gets routed to your site. You in turn make money by selling your products to the prospective customers directed to your site by clicking on the banner.

The choice of website where the banner ad will be displayed is critical to the success and effectiveness of the banner advertising. Appropriate research must be carried out to ensure that the website where you propose to place your banner ad is visited by your target audience.

Using banner ads on the net:
- Increases traffic to your site
- Gives you an opportunity to convert a surfer to your buyer
- Helps your business to reach widespread audience
- Helps branding and increases chances of customers choosing your brand over your competitor's brand

Banner adverts although less popular now, are still quite effective and low cost way to market your business on the Internet. Popular banner exchange services include click4click.com. "Banner Network" is the leader of banner exchange services.

Types of Banner Ads
Banner advertising is a great way to brand your company and generate traffic to your website. Naturally, there are several different types of banner ads:
- Banner Exchanges
  This is the most common type of advertising. When you place a banner on your site, for every two that are seen on your site, one of your banners is displayed on someone else's site.
- Cost Per Impression

Using cost per impression, you provide a banner on someone's website and pay a small fee every time someone sees it (i.e. visits the website hosting).

- Pay Per Click
  The name is self-explanatory. You pay a small fee when someone clicks on your banner.
- Keyword Ads
  This form of banner advertising involves specifying keywords that relate to your ad, your business, and your customers. The placement of your ad is designed to coordinate with user searchbased keyword usage.

Banner advertising campaign
- Banner ad hosting
- Banner ad exchange
- Banner marketing

Measuring the effectiveness of your banner ads
Depending on the program or programs you use to create and post your ads, there are many ways to assess the effectiveness of your banner ads. Most programs allow you to measure the conversion rates of your ads. Google's Adword, for example, lets you measure the number of impressions your keywords generate and it also lets you measure the number of clicks generated by each impression.

If you have a large budget for advertising, it is also possible to have professional teams monitor and measure the effectiveness of your banner ads and make regular efforts to increase your company's online exposure.

Hiring professional banner advertisers
Many companies offer package deals for advertising; to make the process as simple as possible. After all, if your webpage is not made available through search engines, its only function will be as an online business card. You won't generate any new leads.

The advantage of hirng progessional banner advertisers is that they can provide a high degree of focus to get your website placed online, ranked within the first pages of search engine results. Properly deployed search engine results are by far and away the best way to increase leads, growth, and sales for your business. Graphic design is often put to better effect by professional advertisers and generates more traffic.

Many package deals for banner advertising also give you the opportunity to revamp your website and optimize your content for keyword efficiency.

The best strategy for finding professional advertisers is often to conduct a general web search. Be sure to look for package deals as these tend to offer a full range of benefits for your business and, more particularly, for your business.

5) Affiliate Marketing

Like in the traditional businesses in which you make "associates" to sell your products for a commission, you can have "affiliates" on the net selling your products through their websites for a commission.

The affiliates have the information about your products and services on their websites for the surfers of their websites. If a surfer attempts to have more information on the same and click on the specific product or service link they are routed to your website wherein they can continue and choose to make a purchase. Amazon.com is known for its world famous Associate Program.

This "routing" is tracked and the owner of the website from where the link originated is given "credits" or simply speaking is paid a commission as he has assisted the sale of your product. The commission can be anywhere between 5 to 20% of the sale and depends upon the nature of products, the parent company and product pricing.

Who can be an affiliate?
Any website which has the confidence to divert visitors to the parent business's website is eligible to become an affiliate irrespective of its size and turnover.

Who can start an affiliate program?
Any company or business trying to expand, take advantage of other website's traffic and have multiple sale points all across the web normally goes ahead to start an affiliate program.

How do you get your own affiliate?
You have an option of either starting up your own affiliate program or join an existing one and then branch out. You would need to pay for both. If you want to start your own affiliate program you would need to buy the software that will help you manage your program by keeping statistics of total clicks, number of visitors, leads, purchases, individual traffic from all affiliates, payments due, and so on.

On the other hand, joining an existing program would mean that you would have the management taken care of by third party including having your banner ads and links distributed to your affiliates. The affiliate programs you join will let you (mostly) make your affiliates and link to other websites interested in linking to you.

How do you link affiliates to your website?
There are various ways you can have your affiliates' link to your site and route visitors.

The first and foremost is a banner ad.
1. Banner – A banner is the easiest to recognize and can have both text and graphics with good use of color and text effects. Visitors can click on this banner and land up to your home page.

2. Text links – This is another method of routing visitors on your affiliates' website to yours. You can have your link in the content of your affiliate site, clicking on which, the visitors land up on your site. This is a subtler form of advertising that a banner which might get too loud.

You can think of more innovative measures to invite surfers to your website.

How are the affiliates paid?
PPC: You can choose to pay your affiliates by the number of surfers who visit their website and are routed to yours by clicking on the "Affiliate Button" on your affiliate's website. If you pay as per pay per click, you will pay your affiliate according to the total number of visitors he sent across to your site.

Pay Per Lead – PPC has a basic flaw that even if an affiliate of yours does route visitors to you, the visitors may just surf around and might not actually buy anything from your site. However, the very fact they clicked the link and visited your website gives ample proof that they in one way or the other were interested in your product, but could not take a buying decision immediately. You would surely like to have contact details of these visitors whom you can contact from time to time to promote your products.

You can collect the contact addresses of these visitors routed to your site by your affiliate by making them fill an enquiry form at your website. This way you get a lead for your sales team to take further action.

In Pay Per Lead method you pay your affiliate on the number of visitors it diverted to your site, but for those who actually filled up the form and left their contact address even though if they did not buy anything for now.

Pay Per Sale – In this method of determining payment, you pay according to the purchases made by the visitors routed to your website by your affiliate. You don't pay for visiting, and you don't pay for leaving details. A sale is what matters and you agree to pay a percentage on the total sales made to your affiliate.

You may choose to pay your affiliates again if the customers they originally sent make repeat purchase as well. This is called Residual Payment Program and ensures a certain sum of money to the affiliate while you make customers for lifetime.

However you will need to keep a hawk's eye on the number of visitors:
- ✓ clicking on your banner ad at affiliate's website
- ✓ clicking on your link at the affiliate's website
- ✓ leaving their contact address and preferences
- ✓ actually making a purchase

It is very important to know as it will help you determine the payments to be made to your various affiliates. It will also help you compare and contrast the performances of your affiliates and plan accordingly.

If you find the task of managing the statistics too cumbersome, you can consider hiring the services of "affiliate brokers". Affiliate brokers are responsible for managing your affiliates. They take care of your banners and links on affiliate's websites, keep stats of the visitors on your website, total leads generated, total purchases made, and keep an account of the money to be paid to each affiliate along with the data on the individual affiliate performance.

You may also consider using affiliate management software which helps you subscribe to various affiliate programs on the net and measure individual performance and thus give you enough information to decide the best and most profitable ones and plan accordingly.

6) Syndication

There is a limit to the content you can come up with. Moreover it takes immense effort, creativity, and innovation to consistently deliver new content. However, it is important for your website to look fresh with new things coming up regularly.

A rather simple solution to this is syndication.

A number of companies develop content to be distributed for third parties on a regular basis. The content is updated on a regular basis and this updated content is then distributed to the websites using these services. This content is known as syndicated content.

Syndication is used widely in traditional media as well. You must have noticed cartoon strips like "Garfield" in your daily newspaper. Certainly, the newspaper does not write these comic strips. How and why does it appear there? This is because the newspaper in an attempt to provide the readers with some extra content for their enjoyment made an arrangement with the owners of "Garfield" to provide the comic strip. This is a clear-cut case of syndication.

You will frequently come across various examples of this content joint venture in the form of print, television, radio, etc.

Syndicated content may include:
- ✓ Weather forecast report
- ✓ Daily Horoscopes
- ✓ Jokes
- ✓ News on events etc
- ✓ Shopping Bargains
- ✓ Tourist Info
- ✓ World time

A radio or TV channel may give some space for these "syndicated" content. This serves the dual purpose of not having to do all the work in-house as well as serves the need for fresh content by the audience.

This analogy is now extended further as Web Syndication

Web Syndication

Syndication on the web would mean that you make a portion of your website available for other people to access via subscribing and hence authorize other sites to use your content.

Syndication on the web is also pretty much organized and it's easy to incorporate it in your website. A content provider generally prepares content that is appealing to a large section of surfers across various websites.

Benefits of Syndication

Syndication is a way to secure content for your marketing material. It provides benefits of various sorts; content and references for readers. On the website, the receiving site – the site that uses syndicated content – gets greater depth. There's more information and more for the website visitor to read. Syndicated news, general or specific to your business, creates immediacy; archived information creates a body of knowledge that is useful to the reader.

For many sites, syndication also generates new traffic. It is a free and easy form of advertising. Online marketers are familiar with the technique and with its efficiency; online users are more comfortable subscribing to feeds of information,
Additional benefits include the following:
- Users are notified of new content
- Users don't have to actively check for content
- Media files automatically download
- Users don't have to give out their e-mail address to receive feeds
- To unsubscribe, users only need to remove the web feed from their aggregator
- How to establish syndication
- For syndication to work, you must have a feeder to serve as an e-mail program. The syndicated content is sent to your subscribers automatically.

You can fnd a feed reader online, like a webmail account, or else you can download the program you need to your computer and use it offline. Some of these programs are free. Yahoo and MSN offer personalized homepages that function in the same way as feeders. If you have a personal page with either Yahoo or MSN, you receive information updates about news, weather, and stock quotes from syndicate feeders. Firefox browser users and Internet Explore 7.0 users can also use the Live Bookmark functions as a free syndicate feeder tool.

Other free to low-cost feeders include Newsgator, Feed Demon, and Attensa for Microsoft Outlook.

One of the best ways to find a feeder to serve the needs of your business, i.e. one that goes beyond the basic functions of the MyMSN and MyYahoo feeders on the personal pages is to visit the RSS Compendium at http://allrss.com/rssreaders.html.

To secure feeds from most sites, it's necessary to look for the subscriptions or feed options on the source websites. Most of the time, the links that will take you to the relevant pages are labeled as XML, RSS, and Atom, or indicated by an orange button.

Sites such as Yahoo and Google simply have "add to..." buttons using which you can establish the feed aggregators to your website.

A webfeed is the most basic element of most syndication content online. The webfeed is typically a document based in XML that contains summaries or segments of articles with weblinks to the sources of information. The most common web feed formats are RSS and Atom. One popular definition for RSS is "Really Simple Syndication" as it's very easy to publish syndicated items in these online formats.

Examples of Syndicated Web Content include:

- ✓ Weblogs
- ✓ Podcasts
- ✓ Vlogs
- ✓ mainstream mass media websites

Most online syndicated content is sent in either HTML, JavaScript, or XML. The most common format is XML.

The RSS Format
The RSS format is variously referred to as Really Simple Syndication (RSS 2.0), Rich Site Summary (RSS 0.91 and RSS 1.0), and RDF Site Summary (RSS 0.9 and 1.0). Other, slightly more complex RSS modules are Ecommerce RSS 2.0, Media RSS 2.0, and OpenSearch RSS 2.0.

RSS files look something like this:
```
<?xml version="1.0"?>

<rdf:RDF
xmlns:rdf="http://www.w3.org/1999/02/22-rdf-syntax-ns#"
xmlns="http://purl.org/rss/1.0/">

<channel rdf:about="http://www.xml.com/xml/news.rss">
  <title>XML.com</title>
  <link>http://xml.com/pub</link>
```

\<description\>

The Atom Syndicated Format

Atom Syndication Format is an XML language feed used on websites; Atom Publishing Protocol, known as APP, is an HTTP-based protocol for developing and updating a range of web-resources.

Atom syndicated content looks like this:
\<?xml version="1.0" encoding="utf-8"?\>
\<feed xmlns="http://www.w3.org/2005/Atom"\>
 \<title\>Example Feed\</title\>
 \<subtitle\>A subtitle.\</subtitle\>

Common Syndicated Format

Most web feeds are designed to allow software programs to automatically check for updates. Site owners may use content management systems to publish feeds of recent articles. The feeds, picked up by software programs, are downloaded by the websites and feeder reader programs that allow subscribers to view the content.

The most common forms of feeds are full-text articles, excerpts, summaries, and links to other content.

RSS Content Versus Atom Content Syndications

Some syndicated content do not run well in RSS format. Atom format was developed to overcome this problem.

Some things you should know about RSS and Atom:
- RSS 2.0 may contain either plain text or escaped HTML
- Atom allows the inclusion of non-textual content
- RSS is widely used; Atom 1.0 is not
- RSS 2.0 only allows you to use either the full text or the synopsis in the description of the syndication whereas Atom 1.0 allows you to include both a summary and the full text content.

The good news is, it's every easy to outsource this process and most small businesses benefit from doing just that. On the other hand, knowing the basics will help you address concerns and perhaps even discover new and better ways to use syndication to help your business.

Aggregators

To receive syndicated feeds on your website, whether you use RSS or Atom format, you need to have an aggregator on your website. An aggregator is a type of software that can read the web feeds sent to your site by the syndicated content site.

Having an aggretator means you don't have to check websites for updates yourself. The content on your site is updated automatically. Once you subscribe to a feed of syndicated content, your aggregator will check for new content from that feed as often as you determine it is necessary. You can set your aggregator to check for updates every week, every day, or every hour, for example.

Although you can install aggregator features on your website, sites such as MyYahoo and personalized Google sites have built-in aggregators.

An aggregator provides a view of the syndicated content in a single browser display or desktop application. Such applications are also referred to as RSS readers, feed readers, feed aggregators, news readers and search aggregators.

Having an aggregator in your site would mean:

- ✓ You don't have to check for regular updates. Aggregator does it automatically at regular intervals
- ✓ It's a user driven software and checks proactively for updates. This saves you the trouble of receiving loads of emails from syndicated sites and their associated risks like spam, virus, etc
- ✓ No need for user intervention

At present, there are both online and offline versions of aggregators. Online versions are generally provided by particular websites and internet portals as a free service. Most use RSS format and allow users to check for updated feeds manually.

The success of the technology comes from two perspectives:
1. A large amount of online content can be put together in a short period of time and that is what search engines like;
2. The advertising capabilities can be enormous as the ad content can be targeted and delivered very quickly.

Aggregators that work offline and are installed on the user's computer are designed to control subscription and supervise RSS feeds selected by the user. The graphic user interface of this type of software is normally a three-panel composition- communication software like for instance an email program. Publication is made through web-servers so that global access is possible. Additional features are often available so that you can integrate your content feeds with audio players, blog editors, internet browsers, and e-mail clients.

A search engine aggregator is a type of metasearch engine which gathers results from multiple search engines simultaneously through RSS search results. It combines user specified search feeds giving the user the same level of control over content as a general aggregator or news aggregator they might use to install content on their website.

Soon after the introduction of RSS, sites began publicising their search results in parameterized RSS feeds. Search aggregators are an increasingly popular way to take advantage of the power of multiple search engines with a flexibility not seen in traditional metasearch engines. To the end user, a search aggregator may appear to be just a customizable search engine and the use of RSS may be completely hidden. However, the presence of RSS is directly responsible for the existence of search aggregators and a critical component in the behind-the-scenes technology.

A search aggregator typically allows users to select two or more search engines. The aggregator performs a specified query on a number of different sites. The user enters the query into the search aggregator and it generates the required URL by inserting the query into a format that is feeded two or more search engines.

Clouds
Although this method of acquiring syndicated content is quite expensive, for some websites, it's worthwhile having a cloud system; a service that notifies your site's aggregator of updates to a feed.

Podcasting
You can distribute audio content over I-Pod (the digital audio player). This process is called Podcasting. The content can be played on any standard MP3 player – on a computer or off. The phenomenon is now extremely popular; podcasting is the latest marketing tool with an online base.

The concept of podcasting was suggested as early as 2000 and its technical components were available by 2001. Podcasting was first implemented in the program Radio Userland. In 2003 regular podcasts started showing up on well-known Web sites and software support spread.

Podcasting content is surely a niche. People who are genuinely interested in the subject and benefit from the same download it. From a marketing perspective, content reaches your target customers in an interesting format.

You might want to incorporate some third party content which is updated daily to add some freshness to the existing content on your website. The website looks maintained and holds interest of the surfer by offering new things.

The content provider then acknowledges the existence of that file by referencing it in the feed. The feed is a list of the URLs by which episodes of the show may be accessed. This list is usually published in RSS format (although Atom can also be used). It provides other information, such as publish date, titles, and accompanying text descriptions of the series and each of its episodes. The feed may contain entries for all episodes in the series, but is typically limited to a short list of the most recent episodes. Standard podcasts consist of a feed from one author. More recently, multiple authors have been able to contribute episodes to a single podcast feed using concepts such as public podcasting and social podcasting.

The content provider posts the feed on a webserver. The location is known as the feed URI (or, perhaps more often, feed URL). The content provider makes this feed URI known to the intended audience.

A consumer uses an aggregator, sometimes called a podcatcher or podcast receiver to subscribe and manage their feeds.

A podcast specific aggregator is usually an always on; it's generally a program that starts when the computer is turned on. It continues to run in the background and manages a set of feed URIs added by the user and downloads each at a specified interval, such as every two hours. If the feed data has substantively changed from when it was previously checked (or if the feed was just added to the application's list), the program determines the location of the most recent item and automatically downloads it to the user's computer.

Perhaps only 20% of podcasts are actually consumed on portable media players; 80% are consumed on the PC onto which they are downloaded. Some applications, such as iTunes, also automatically make the newly downloaded episodes available to a user's portable media player.

The downloaded episodes can then be played, replayed, or archived as with any other computer file.

To conserve bandwidth, users may opt to search for content using an online podcast directory. Some directories allow people to listen online and initially become familiar with the content provided from an RSS feed before deciding to subscribe. For most broadband users, bandwidth is generally not a major consideration; it could fairly be stated that podcasting itself is a technology that came with the increases in global bandwidth and broadband popularity.

The initial appeal of podcasting was that it allowed individuals and businesses to distribute their own radio shows. The system quickly became used in a wide variety of other ways, including distribution of school lessons, official and unofficial audio tours of museums, conference meeting alerts and updates, and by police departments to distribute public safety messages.
Given the popular of podcasts and their growing presence onlne, it's easy for businesses to find uses for this technology.

Autocasting
Autocasting is an automated form of podcasting that allows bloggers and blog readers to generate audio versions of text blogs from RSS feeds. Autocasting software uses XML parsers, TTS (text-to-speech) engines, and audio conversion utilities to convert text blogs

into audio files that can be placed on a blog for download, synchronized to a portable audio device, or played on a desktop computer.

Stream Media
Streaming media is heard or viewed asit is being delivered. The streaming is more a property of the delivery system than the medium itself. The distinction is usually applied to media that are distributed over computer networks. Most delivery systems are either inherently streaming or non-streaming. Radio and television are inherently streaming whereas books, video cassettes, and audio CDs are examples of non-streaming media.

The word stream is used as a verb, meaning to deliver streaming media. It most often refers to the delivery of a media onto computers via the internet, a concept dating back the the earliest days of the computer.

Academic experiments in the 1970s proved out the basic concepts and feasibility of streaming media on computers. During the late 1980s, consumer-grade computers became powerful enough to display various media. However, computer networks were still limited, and media was usually delivered over non-streaming channels, such as CD-ROMs.

Establishing stream media on a website – whether it's syndicated news content or a promotional advertisement your company has developed – depends largely on your software and the size of the file.

If you want to integrate stream media onto your website, the best approach, to ensure that you don't have any problems and to ensure that your customers don't have problems viewing your content, it's best to hire a professional web designer.

7) Blogging

What is a blog?
A blog is a website in the form of an online journal; the latest entry appearing first. On most blogs, content is added daily, sometimes several times a day. There are hundreds of blogs getting added everyday in the *blogosphere*. Various blogs on the Internet are connected to each other and hence information added to any blog can travel really fast and encompass the web in a very short time.

As of now there are a minimum 60 million active blogs on the Internet, tracked by Technorati.

Blogging and Social Media
Social media describes the online tools and platforms that people use to share opinions, insights, experiences, and perspectives with each other. At present, it takes many different forms, including text, images, audio, and video, with the most popular online tools being blogs, message boards, podcasts, wikis, and vlogs.

For businesses, large and small, social media, blogging in particular, is an excellent tool. A number of ventures using blogging and other forms of social meria have proven the significance of this media.

After the 2006 Oscars, for example, the global non-profit organization, Oxfam, used a social media campaign to auction off Keira Knightley's dress. Operating on a low budget, Oxfam hired a social media agency to reach out to Keira Knightley fan websites as well as blogs and message boards for celebrity gossip. The auction raised $7,855 and about 79 bidders competed, with 2,500 watching the auction on eBay in the final seconds. Bloggers helped generate offline publicity for Oxfam, including over 150 traditional media mentions across the U.S.

Volvo, in an effort to promote the release of Pirates of the Caribbean 2, started a campaign in which people worldwide could hunt for "Pirates Treasure". The treasure was a pirate-themed Volvo SUV. To promote the contest they allowed people to share tips, clues and even poems through a dedicated blog hosted by MSN Spaces.

Volvo was able to get over 30,000 people involved, leading up to and during the release of the film.

How do you start a blog?
There are many types of software that can be used – bought or downloaded – to establish and run a blog. The most popular software programs are:
WordPress,
blogger
LiveJournal
DreamHost

How does blogging help your business?
Although blogging is a great way for people to keep friends and family informed about their daily lives – a very common use – blogs are an excellent marketing tool for businesses.

In January 2005, Fortune Magazine published a list featuring eight bloggers that 'business people' could not ignore. The list features here in it's original form:
1. Peter Rojas
2. Xeni Jardin
3. Ben Trott
4. Mena Trott
5. Jonathan Schwartz
6. Jason Goldman
7. Robert Scoble
8. Jason Calacanis

These individuals have proven that blogs are a great way to market a business, generate leads, and make sales. Blogs can be a running commentary on a particular hot topic or simply a collection of recent news or personal experiences. The written style generally differs from one blog to the next.

How can a corporate use blog for advertising?

You can find out or start a blog that talks about a subject relevant to your business – this is a great way to promote your business. You can have plenty of opportunity to mention your products and services.

Many companies hire writers to provide content – everything from news bites to feature length articles – to promote their business. While input from a professional writer is not required, it is useful to check out other company blogs and do a bit of research on what draws people to this form of communication if you intend to use it yourself.

Few relevant web sources are:
- ✓ Marketing Blog
- ✓ Popdex
- ✓ eatonweb.com
- ✓ Weblogs.com
- ✓ Blogging Network
- ✓ blogger.com
- ✓ Google Directory : On The Web : Web Logs
- ✓ Yahoo : Directory: Computers and Internet : Web Logs

Types of Blogs

At this time, there are estimated to be more than 60 million blogs online. Not surprisingly, there are many types of blogs. Everything from political blogs to travel blogs, leval blogs to photoblogs, corporate blogs to vlogs.

Some of the most common commercial types of blogs will be discussed here.

The vast majority of blogs are not commercial. Most bloggers don't necessarily have an interest in making money. They may make a small profit from their blog by using targeted banner advertising, but the majority of bloggers don't have commercial interest they are seeking to promote for themselves. That said, many full-time bloggers are paid to promote merchandise and services of particular companies in the bulk of their submissions.

A typical blog entry tends to include the following elements:
- Title of the article
- Body Content of the article
- URL linking the blog summary to the full article
- Post Date of the original date and time of publication

Some blogs feature comments, categories or tags to attract search engines, and trackback or pingback links to other sites that relate to a particular entry.

Comments are a very popular way to provide discussion on blog entries. Readers can comment on a post, whether it's to make a correction or simply express an opinion. This feature is a great way to discuss about your business online and general exposure.

Several researchers have analyzed how blogs become popular. The two most common measures are citations and affiliation. It takes time for a blog to become popular through blogrolls but permalinks can boost popularity more quickly, and are perhaps more indicative of popularity and authority than blogrolls.

Blogs are also given rankings by Technorati based on the amount of incoming links and Alexa Internet based on the web hits of Alexa Toolbar users. In August 2006, Technorati listed the most linked-to blog as that of Chinese actress Xu Jinglei and the most-read blog as group-written Boing Boing.

The Chinese media reported that the blog of Xu Jinglei received more than 50 million page views, making it perhaps the most popular blog in the world. Mid-year, 2006, Xu Jinglei's blog also had the most incoming links of any blogs on the Internet.

Some institutions see blogging as a means of "getting around the filter" and pushing messages directly to the public. Some critics worry that bloggers respect neither copyright nor the role of the mass media in presenting society with credible news.

8) Google & Froogle

What is Google?
Google is a popular search engine tool employed by World Wide Web users. The engine is a tool for scanning and organizing web pages that have relevance to keywords submitted by the user.

The search engine web page, www.google.com, was launched in 1998.

What is Froogle?
In December, 2002, Google formally announced Froogle a price comparision service. Unlike most of these types of services, Froogle doesn't charge fees for listings or accept payment for placement of ads. What's more, the company doesn't require a commission on sales. Any company can submit a product on this feed by sending information via AdWord.

Search results are ordered by relevance or price. You can also search for items in specific online stores.

In addition to Froogle, there are a number of other online price comparision services businesses should be aware of:

Kelkoo

NexTag
Price.com
PriceAsk.com
PriceGrabber.com
Shopping.com
ShopWiki
Shopzilla
AuctionSHARK

These sites all serve pretty much the same purpose as Froogle. Some charge fees for listings and advertisements. Depending on your overall business strategy, the fees may be worth the exposure these sites can bring to your business.

9)LinkBaiting

Introduction
The internet is a great tool and its range is improving all the time. Email marketing, blogging, and syndication, while they are great ways to expand the horizons of your business and draw wanted attention, these are strategies that many businesses and competitors use, and have used for some time. One of the most effective marketing tools is not anything like a sales letter, or sales copy injected into an online blog. It's not even a video advertisement syndicated and posted on websites.

What You Need to Know About Linkbaiting
One of the best ways to market your business is simply to provide a benefit to your customers that gets them talking about and looking at the right things.

In the last couple of years, even less, linkbait has been spread all across the Internet; identified as an innovative marketing technique that is both new and somewhat controversial. But linkbaiting is above all a cheap and efficient way to generate traffic for your website.

The more links your website has, the more business you generate. Of course, there are lots of different ways to get links to your site. Even the cheap methods are very effective. Providing content rich pages, submitting articles and press releases to various distribution sites and trading links will generate interest in your site. These things will interest your customer base, but nothing works quite as well as linkbait.

A linkbait is specifically generated content designed to be of interest to others. The idea is that visitors to your site, drawn by the link bait, will voluntarily create links back to your website without you having to ask it of them. Much like a viral videos, linkbaits can spread around the Internet at the speed of light. It spreads without you having to make any effort.

The key to linkbait is to create content that is short and yet very interesting and engaging:

Controversial opinions

Subjects that lead to heated debate are always good for generating traffic. Controversial topics on which people can comment will certainly get attention drawn to your site.No matter what industry you are in, there will be subjects that lead to heated debates. If you post a blog on to your website that features controversial content readers alert others to what you have to say and then additionally will visit your website.

Sensational stories

Find a new angle to promote your site by publishing stories with a sentimental edge.

Freebies

People like nothing better than perks. If you can provide free information, free tips, or even a free service, you're likely to generate interest in your site. Free stuff is perfect linkbait.

Humor

Laughter is the way to most people's hearts. If you can find a way to make people laugh, whether it's a humorous blog, jokes, funny videos, anything like that, it's highly probably that your website will receive high and regular traffic volumes.

Trivia

Most people find trivias irrestistable. Interesting and odd facts and figures are great linkbait because these often end up on other people's blogs. Take MySpace as an example and you'll see lots of pages where people have posted favorite links to unusual information and quizzes they found in obscure places on the Internet.

Contests and Games

Another great way to get traffic is by starting a contest or a game on your site. Look for the worst Halloween costume or the best looking baby from among your visitors. Word will spread and you could find your site becoming so popular that major Internet news sites pick them up.

Internet Marketing Companies

As you may not have time to develop new ideas and you may not have the capacity to bring your ideas to life, hiring an internet marketing company is probably something you should seriously consider. Internet marketing companies are very much focused on taking your ideas and information to fashion them into finished products, idea for marketing. They can also develop linkbait from the ground up that will explode the growth of links to your website.

Chapter 12: Case Studies

Overview

One of the best ways to understand the advantage of the internet for a business in today's world is to review examples of online business successes. This chapter aims to introduce some of the major internet successes – individuals and corporations – that have achieved great things by applying logical and workable strategies to conquer the internet.

Alex Mandossian, Online Marketing Expert

First on the list of dot.com turn-around experts is the marketing executive, Alex Mandosssian, who held the position of Chief Marketing Officer at Robell Research, Inc., a Madison Avenue market research firm, in the 1990s.

Mandossian is recognized for having developed and distributed infomercials such as 'Thigh Master' for Suzanne Somers, RONCO Food Dehydrator for Ron Popeil, Players Club International for Telly Savalas, Ray Stevens Comedy Video Classics, and Time Life's Wild Animal Video Series.

More recently, Alex has helped his clients generate millions of dollars in sales from TV spots, infomercials, QVC, Home Shopping Network, catalogs, direct mail, Internet marketing, and postcards.

Online, Alex Mandossian has earned a reputation for being one of the best copywriters, speakers, teleseminar conversion consultants, and traffic conversion consultants in the Internet industry.

He is also the co-founder of AskDatabase, AudioGenerator, and InstantVideoGenerator and the first user of Audio Postcards, Video Postcards, and online surveys to capture more sales and profits, faster, better, and easier than ever.

Although there are many lessons to be learned from an individual as multi-talented as this one, it is his efforts to know his audience that are most interesting and impressive. Audio Postcards, Video Postcards, and online surveys should, if possible, be used by every business online.

Corey Rudl

Among the Internet gurus of the age, Rudl stands out as a true genius.
Corey Rudl had
- ✓ 4 Online Businesses
- ✓ $6.6 million of sales generated in online sales per year
- ✓ Over 60000 affiliates
- ✓ Over 1.8 million website hits per month

A marketing expert and e-commerce pioneer, Corey started his first online business in 1994 with a start-up investment of just $25. He successfully turned that small investment into a multi-million-dollar business. His secret was results-driven Internet marketing strategies.

In respond to the demand for his online business acumen, Corey founded The Internet Marketing Center, now a multi-million-dollar corporation. The Internet Marketing Center shares its Internet marketing strategies and software solutions with countless entrepreneurs and businesses worldwide.

From this example of online success, it's important to understand the need to modify; to test and improve marketing strategies. Corey maintained his success with online businesses by testing new strategies on a daily basis. He developed the ability to forecast market trends and predict the "next big thing", strategically placing himself to cash in on it.

His Internet Marketing course, "Insider Secrets to Marketing Your Business on the Internet," is one of the most successful and useful "How To" guides in print today.

Derek Gehl
A colleage of Corey Rudl, Derek Gehl is now the president of the Internet Marketing Center.

For invaluable online marketing tips and strategies, visit to two sites featured below:
http://www.marketingtips.com/
http://www.auctiontips.com/

Joe Vitale

Joe Vitale is most widely known for his strength in creating, analyzing and reviewing ads, flyers, news releases and sales letters. Joe currently has more than 500 clients worldwide and the list is growing daily. Vitale is also known for his ability to put together web sites that put people into "buying trances." and this whole technique is based on his latest ebook called "Hypnotic Marketing."

Joe has written many books and is the producer of the extremely popular Nightingale-Conant audiotape collection, "The Power of Outrageous Marketing!"

Joe also produced "CyberWriting: How to Promote Your Product or Service Online" (Without Being Flamed), "Turbocharge Your Writing"(1988), "The AMA Complete Guide to Small Business Advertising.", "There's A Customer Born Every Minute: P.T. Barnum's Secrets for Business Success"(1998), "The AMA Complete Guide to Small Business Advertising"(1996)

His most recent book, co-authored with Jo Han Mok, is *The E-Code: 47 Secrets for Making Money Online Almost Instantly.*

He is one of the five top marketing specialists in the world today, as well as being the world's first hypnotic writer.

In addition to gaining great insight about marketing and online business advertising from his numerous published projects, it's s good idea to check out some of his opins, blogs, and the like to get a really good handle on his very particular and very successful style of marketing.

TURN AROUND BUSINESSES

The list of individuals who have become renowned as online marketing experts is extensive; far too extensive to cover in one book. That said, a Google search should bring you more information and additional names to check out.

Far more important in this context is to look at the big business players; companies that have affected a dramatic success by implementing online marketing strategies.

Gerneral Motors
- Famous for its corporate blog: General Motors FastLane
- One of the first companies to publish a blog written by a Senior Executive
- Uses its blog to correct biased or inaccurate reports in the mainstream media
- Balances priorities for the blog: answering questions that seem important while staying focused on their primary goal of promoting and discussing company products.
- Blog attracts 7,500 visitors per day; receives an average of 70 comments per post.

GM started their blog in October 2004. They started small so that they could perfect the process of creating news and getting reactions from customers. They focused on generating different conversation topics, maintaining good content. GM's blog doesn't use copywriters to control or push discussion topics.

A team of six writers are responsible for the content. There's also someone responsible for the editing.

The advantages of a webblog for your businesses:
- Opportunity to talk to your customers
- Design is simple
- You control how often you post
- Great, informal way to promote your product.

National Association of Manufacturers
- 10 year old website
- Started a blog within 14 months
- Unique visitors to the NAM blog surpassed visitors to the mainsite
- The goal is to improve the image of manufacturers

- Blog helped to build a 'cutting-edge' reputation
- Traffic grows about 20% per month
- 14,000 visits per week
- Blog drives 10% of the regular internet traffic
- In 14 months, the blog has received over 1,200 comments
- Every Saturday, the company publishes a video on their "CoolStuffBeingMade" section, which is aimed at kids

Although its value was initially questioned, the blog is now an integral part of the business, updated several times a day.

The goal was to revamp NAM's communication, make it more engaging to new readers, and ultimately building an online community.

Summary
If you really want to build a strong internet business opportunity – an opportunity strong enough to turn your business around if it's in trouble – you have to be able to find or build your own positioning. Positioning is basically a niche to attract your website visitors.

Big companies spend millions in market research to find a unique position. In this area of business, however, money can't necessarily buy you the answers. Many of the biggest corporations out there still fail to find their niche. The good news for small business owners: in some ways, it's easier to develop positioning for a small business. It seems to be advantages for business when a website has a personal feel to it, the kind of feel achieved when the site is literally the result of the entrepreneur's personal effort.

So why a unique positioning is important? The stronger your positioning or brand image, the stronger your relationship with your target audience. The more you'll sell.The strong positioning website will get targeted traffic easier, because the visitor will see at once, whether this internet business opportunity is for him or not.

Okay, we agree that a unique positioning is important, but how to get one? Let us keep it simple. The best way is to give your internet business opportunity like your own faces, make it like you want: colours, template, copystyle, products, services and so on. When you prepare your website, it is like a discussion with your customer. Try to think as he does. Or try to be a customer of your own website.

We strongly believe that when you honestly want to help your customers, you will succeed. An internet business opportunity is a 100 % service business. Take it personally and build unique positioning with great service. Express your willingness to help. Answer all customer emails professionally and rapidly. Ask all the time, whether you could help more. Soon the word will spread and your brand will get the positioning as the service website, which really cares about the customers. You have visited many, many websites. How many of them has a good service? The answer is: quite rare ones.

The service positioning is a unique way, because no one simply can copy you. You are in a way expanding your personality into your website! This works! All decisions are made by feelings but told rationally. Now you have built an emotional relationship with your customers. That means trust.

Your internet business opportunity has got to be unique. The most important thing is, whether your target audience sees it as an unique one. And this is the process, which you can influence. You can conquer the position of, let us say the best service home business site, in the thoughts of your audience by repeating your service message every time you promote your site.Make it in the form of a positioning slogan.

We want to give you a list, when we go through the positioning issues:

1.In what way is my website unique?(widest range of products, most beautiful one)
2.Describe the uniqueness.
3.Does my site offer value?
4.Does my website express quality?
5.Do I offer 30 or 60 days money back quarantee?
6.Am I reliable, do I build trust?
7.Do I answer all emails within a day?
8.Do I express a willingness to help a visitor?
9.Do I express that I will be in business long term?

Summary: Put your own personality on fire, and you will build a great positioning for your internet business opportunity!

Further Resources

BOOKS

Business Turnaround
"Streetwise Small Business Turnaround: Revitalizing Your Struggling or Stagnant Enterprise" by Marc Kramer

"Successful Corporate Turnarounds
by Eugene F. Finkin

"Harvard Business Review on Turnarounds"
Harvard Business Review

Business Turnaround and Bankruptcy Kit
by John Ventura

"The Six Month Fix: Adventures in Rescuing Failing Companies"
by Sutton and Gary Sutton

Business Plans
"Adams Streetwise Business Plans"
Adams Media Corporation

"Business Plans Kit For Dummies"
by Steven D. Peterson, Peter E. Jaret, and Barbara Findlay Schenck

Writing a Convincing Business Plan
by Arthur R. DeThomas Ph.D. and Lin Grensing-Pophal

"The Successful Business Plan: Secrets and Strategies"
by Rhonda Abrams and Eugene Kleiner

"How to Write A .com Business Plan: The Internet Entrepreneur's Guide to Everything You Need to Know About Business Plans and Financing Options"
by Joanne Eglash

Using the Internet for Business
"Getting Rich In Your Underwear: How To Start And Run A Profitable Home-Based Business"
by Peter, I Hupalo

"Internet Riches: The Simple Money-making Secrets of Online Millionaires"
by Scott C. Fox

"Starting an Online Business All-in-One Desk Reference For Dummies
by Shannon Belew and Joel Elad

"Starting an Online Business For Dummies"
by Greg Holden

"Legal Environment of Business and Online Commerce"
by Henry R. Cheeseman

Unofficial Guide to Starting a Business Online
by Jason R. Rich

"Starting a Yahoo! Business For Dummies"
by Rob Snell

"The Everything Online Business Book"
by Rob Liflander

"Online Marketing Success Stories: Insider Secrets, from the Experts Who Are Making Millions on the Internet Today"
by Rene V. Richards

"Contemporary Business Law and Online Commerce Law"
by Henry R. Cheeseman

"The Home-Based Bookstore: Start Your Own Business Selling Used Books on Amazon, eBay or Your Own Web Site by Steve Weber"
ONLINE RESOURCES

BusinessTown
http://www.businesstown.com
Featuring Articles, Tips, and Links relating to Businesses Online

References

Advertising Networks, Wikipedia.com
http://en.wikipedia.org/wiki/Advertising_network

Dr. Wilson's Plain-Spoken Guide to Search Engine Optimization (2006 Edition)
http://www.wilsonweb.com/ebooks/seo.htm

The E-Mail Marketing Handbook
(Second Edition) 2005
http://www.wilsonweb.com/ebooks/handbook.htm

Internet Marketing, Wikipedia.com.
http://en.wikipedia.org/wiki/Online_marketing

Online Advertising, Wikipedia.com
http://en.wikipedia.org/wiki/Online_advertising

Planning Your Internet Marketing Strategy: A Doctor Ebiz Guide
http://www.wilsonweb.com/plan/

Search Engine, Wikipedia.com
http://en.wikipedia.org/wiki/Search_engine

Search Engine Optimization, Wikipedia.com
http://en.wikipedia.org/wiki/Search_engine_optimization

Web Banner, Wikipedia.com
http://en.wikipedia.org/wiki/Banner_ads

Web Marketing Today
http://www.wilsonweb.com/

Web Traffic, Wikipedia.com
http://en.wikipedia.org/wiki/Web_traffic